How to Open and Operate
a Financially Successful

REDESIGN, REDECORATING, *and* HOME STAGING

Business

With Companion CD-ROM

Mary Larsen
With Teri B. Clark

How to Open and Operate a Financially Successful Redesign, Redecorating, and Home Staging Business: With Companion CD-ROM

Copyright © 2007 Atlantic Publishing Group, Inc.
1405 SW 6th Avenue • Ocala, Florida 34471 • Phone 800-814-1132 • Fax 352-622-1875
Web site: www.atlantic-pub.com • E-mail: sales@atlantic-pub.com
SAN Number: 268-1250

ISBN 13: 978-1-60138-023-4 • ISBN 10: 1-60138-023-2

Larsen, Mary, 1969-
How to open & operate a financially successful redesign, redecorating & and home staging buisness, with companion CD-ROM / by Mary Larsen.
    p. cm.
"With companion CD-ROM."
ISBN-13: 978-1-60138-023-4 (alk. paper)
ISBN-10: 1-60138-023-2
1. Home staging--United States. 2. House selling--United States. 3. Interior decoration--United States. 4. New business enterprises--United States. I. Title. II. Title: How to open and operate a financially successful redesign, redecorating, and home staging buisness.

HD259.L37 2008
333.33'830973--dc22
                    2007039186

Printed on Recycled Paper

Interior Layout: Vickie Taylor • vtaylor@atlantic-pub.com

Printed in the United States

"Mary has a passion for this industry and her talent shines. The information she has to share is such a gift. This book will become a resource for many years to come."

Margie Nance
President
Custom Home Furnishings Academy
http://www.chfschool.com/

"So you know you can decorate - but do you know how to make money while providing the service? This book will help ensure your business success while you follow your decorating passion."

JoAnne Lenart-Weary
Founder
One Day Decorating and The Society for Design Professionals
www.onedaydecorating.com
www.TheSDP.com

"This book covers everything from A - Z to help a person launch a successful design business. The chapter on marketing is exceptional! A very easy read and well thought out book."

Debbie Green
National speaker and founder of
Minutes Matter and Minutes Matter Studio
www.minutesmatterstudio.com

"Mary's book is just the resource needed for this industry. So many talented decorators launch with excitement and fail to manage the business side with a clear plan. As a National Trainer with SDP I look forward to using this book in my training center. Mary Larsen has done an excellent job at keeping it informative and REAL! "

Laure Gill
Award Winning Decorating Professional and
TV personality on TLC's Property Ladder
Owner, Reborn Rooms Interiors & Training
www.rebornrooms.com

"I have experienced first hand the value of Mary's tips and techniques in three homes. Now this book will be a treasured addition to your library. It is a must read if you're even thinking about starting your own redesign business. It's all here and simply brings order to the chaos of starting a business. No more "where do I begin?" Now the only question is "when!"

Barbara Giemza
Founder
Executive Suite Partners, LLC
www.wegrowwisdom.com

"I have been an interior designer and redesigner for a number of years, and it is a complicated business. Mary's book is written in such a way that it is easy to reference and worded so anyone can understand this complex business of design. Kudos for making it look easy!"

Shelley T. Boe, IRIS
Owner
Design 'n Style
www.designnstyle.com

We recently lost our beloved pet "Bear," who was not only our best and dearest friend but also the "Vice President of Sunshine" here at Atlantic Publishing. He did not receive a salary but worked tirelessly 24 hours a day to please his parents. Bear was a rescue dog that turned around and showered myself, my wife Sherri, his grandparents Jean, Bob and Nancy and every person and animal he met (maybe not rabbits) with friendship and love. He made a lot of people smile every day.

We wanted you to know that a portion of the profits of this book will be donated to The Humane Society of the United States.

–Douglas & Sherri Brown

THE HUMANE SOCIETY
OF THE UNITED STATES ©

The human-animal bond is as old as human history. We cherish our animal companions for their unconditional affection and acceptance. We feel a thrill when we glimpse wild creatures in their natural habitat or in our own backyard.

Unfortunately, the human-animal bond has at times been weakened. Humans have exploited some animal species to the point of extinction.

The Humane Society of the United States makes a difference in the lives of animals here at home and worldwide. The HSUS is dedicated to creating a world where our relationship with animals is guided by compassion. We seek a truly humane society in which animals are respected for their intrinsic value, and where the human-animal bond is strong.

Want to help animals? We have plenty of suggestions. Adopt a pet from a local shelter, join The Humane Society and be a part of our work to help companion animals and wildlife. You will be funding our educational, legislative, investigative and outreach projects in the U.S. and across the globe.

Or perhaps you'd like to make a memorial donation in honor of a pet, friend or relative? You can through our Kindred Spirits program. And if you'd like to contribute in a more structured way, our Planned Giving Office has suggestions about estate planning, annuities, and even gifts of stock that avoid capital gains taxes.

Maybe you have land that you would like to preserve as a lasting habitat for wildlife. Our Wildlife Land Trust can help you. Perhaps the land you want to share is a backyard—that's enough. Our Urban Wildlife Sanctuary Program will show you how to create a habitat for your wild neighbors.

So you see, it's easy to help animals. And The HSUS is here to help.

The Humane Society of the United States
2100 L Street NW
Washington, DC 20037
202-452-1100
www.hsus.org

Author

Dedication

In 2001, I launched my own interior design and redesign business. I researched everything I could get my hands on and found that information for a home-based interior design business was sorely lacking. Never daunted by a difficult task, I pursued my business venture and dove in.

Starting in my area, I contacted people who were doing something similar to what I wanted to do. Luckily for me, the first person I spoke with was Deb Kearney of Woven Materials in Cary, North Carolina. Deb owns a custom window treatment workroom and is a supplier of fabulous trim. She agreed to meet with me, and after some in-depth discussion, she referred me to Linda Tuorto. Linda is the owner of Linda Tuorto Interiors, an interior design firm also located in Cary. Soon after meeting Linda, I secretly declared her my mentor. With the guidance and support of these two amazing women, I was able to move my business forward.

I then became involved in two professional organizations, the Interior Design Society and the Window Coverings Association of America. I met several more women who became part of my incredible support system. Perhaps you see a pattern. There are amazing people all around you who can be of great assistance to you — you just need to go out and find them. I remember how happy I was the first time I was able to share something helpful with these women and return the favor; today we are a great support team for each other.

Margie Nance and JoAnne Lenart-Weary both have been incredibly helpful. So have my close friends — the smartest, funniest women I know — Leesl, Bethie, Cindy, Barb, Susan, Audrey, and the "Girls' Lunch Group."

The old maxim "give and you shall receive" has been used in my business more times than I can count, and I encourage you to run your business with that sentiment, helping others while letting others help you. Teri B. Clark has been instrumental in the development of this book, and we have had a great "give and receive!"

Before I close, I would like to give a never-ending thank-you to my most important support team — my large and ever-growing family. Thank you to my amazing parents, Rose and Dick, and to my wonderful eight brothers and sisters and their spouses and families. To my husband's family and most importantly to his incredible children, Kaylan, Kiera, and Mackenzie — I am blessed to have you in my life. And to my husband Rick, my biggest supporter and the most important of all.

I have learned a tremendous amount about this quirky business called design, a service industry that sells a product. It is truly unique! This book is part of my "giving," and I look forward to hearing from you about how this book has helped you and what great tips you want to share with others.

Here's to Designing Your Success™!

- Mary

Table of

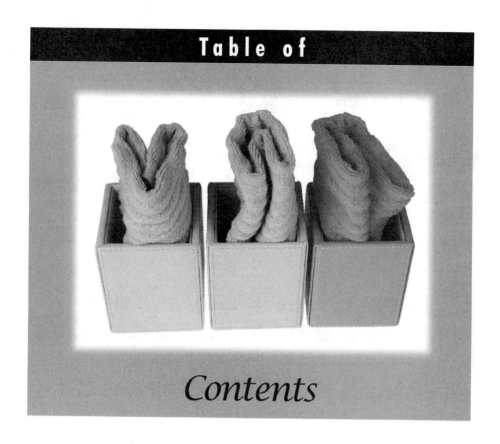

Contents

Introduction

*A*nalysts believe that the cocooning effect following 9/11 caused great growth in all things related to the enjoyment of the home. Indeed, pool builders and retailers have experienced double-digit growth since 2001, and *nesting* — a term coined years ago — was an American buzzword once again.

Such nesting trends explain the huge growth of businesses related to home design. For example, interior design, something once reserved for the "rich and famous," has found its way into virtually every home in America.

A look at the Interior Redesign Industry Specialists (IRIS) Web site (**www.weredesign.com**) gives us insight into the rapidly growing field of redesign. In 1999, IRIS had 19 members. In 2007, there are more than 600 members. Growth also is reflected in the number of redesign shows on HGTV and cable networks, such as *Decorating Cents*, *Design Remix*, and *FreeStyle*.

Home staging has experienced similar advances. The International Association of Home Staging Professionals now has 107 local chapters. Real estate companies, such as ERA, have their agents learn home staging, and the Certified Staging Professionals (CSP) network has increased by 500 members from 2006 to 2007.

Are you planning to become part of this redesign or real estate staging network? During this time of phenomenal growth, these businesses may be worth investigating. If you can answer yes to the following questions, the redesign or home staging business may be just right for you:

- Do you love decorating your home?

- Are you addicted to home decorating shows and magazines?

- Do you know exactly what someone should do to sell his home fast?

- Are you constantly moving your furniture around?

- Do you find yourself decorating for your friends and family for free?

- Do you have a flair for decorating?

Keep in mind, however, that redesign and real estate staging are about more than just having the talent and skills to do the job. The business of the business is the part that can be tricky.

Readers of this book will fall into one of the following categories:

- **Those With a Second Career:** You already have a successful career and are looking for something new. In fact, the design field may be completely unrelated to anything you have ever done before.

- **Those Wishing to Be Their Own Boss:** You want to have more control over your day and how it goes. Being your own boss allows you to be flexible.

- **Those Who Are Business Beginners:** You have started your own business and are finding that the available small-business tools just do not apply to the design industry.

- **Those Who Want to Grow Their Design Business:** You already are fully engaged in your own design business and need sound marketing principles to grow your business further.

- **Those Who Are Curious:** You just want to know what the design industry is all about and find out if you can develop your passion into a thriving business.

No matter which description fits you, this book will be instrumental in your success when it comes to the business side of redesigning and home staging.

In these chapters, you will learn whether you are cut out to be an entrepreneur; what to offer as a redesigner, redecorator, and home stager; what to charge for your services; how to create a simple and formal business plan; how to set up your home office; the legalities of owning a business; how to market; how to give a presentation; the day-to-day workings of your job; and professional design techniques. You will read expert examples and business blunders. You will receive tips, scripts, and templates.

After you are finished with this book, you will be ready to start your own redesign, redecorate, and home staging business. More important, you will be ready to succeed.

Let the journey begin.

Chapter 1

Should You or Should You Not? That Is The Question

A Little History

*B*efore you can determine whether you should start your own **redesign** or **home staging** business, you will need to understand what they are and how they differ.

Redesign was born out of the field of interior design. Average consumers believe the following stereotypes:

- Interior designers are too expensive.

- Interior designers are intimidating and hard to work with.

- Interior designers are going to throw out everything and suggest all new items.

Not every interior designer fits these stereotypes, but the perception does exist, therefore relegating interior design to those with time and money. As people became more interested in staying at home, a newer way to change the interior of homes — one that did not have such negative connotations — emerged. This new field is redesign.

Redesign (redecorating) is the art of using a homeowner's furniture, rugs, wall hangings, and accessories in a way that makes a room the best it possibly can be. Redesign can take a room from boring to beautiful. It is immediate satisfaction and gratification, and the amazing transformation takes only one day.

Home Staging (also known as **Real Estate Staging**) had its beginnings on the West Coast, where real estate pricing varied dramatically from location to location. In the past, realtors focused on the mechanics of selling a home and the administrative and legal aspects and paid little attention to a buyer's perspective. In fact, many realtors still do, leaving any thought of repair or updating in the hands of the homeowner. This is where your home staging business will come into play.

Home staging is much more than cleaning up your home to prepare it for sale. The way someone lives in a home is different from the way someone needs to sell a home. When living in a home, people want to be comfortable and relaxed. They want their home to be a reflection of who they are.

On the other hand, when a home is for sale, the goal is to have every potential buyer think that he or she can live in the home. It is no longer about the homeowner. Instead, it is about the homebuyer. Coupling a designer's eye with the buyer's perspective is what home staging is all about.

Home redesign is for living. Home staging is for selling. Despite their different aims, both take business sense and design skills.

Are You Cut Out to Be an Entrepreneur?

You think you want to become an entrepreneur and start your own design business. Before you can know if you are cut out to be an entrepreneur, however, you have to understand just what an entrepreneur is. That is not quite as simple as it sounds, since the definition has been changing for nearly 100 years.

The first definition was simply someone who invented something. Eventually it turned into someone who owned a business. Neither one of these definitions really got to the heart of entrepreneurship. The best definition, and the one used today, is this:

An entrepreneur is someone who organizes, manages, and assumes the risks for a business or an enterprise.

In this definition the entrepreneur sees an opportunity and builds a business around that opportunity. He or she has a vision and builds around this vision, assuming all the risk.

Debunking Entrepreneurial Myths

Not only have definitions been changing, but also myths have been circulating. Let us examine these myths while putting things into better perspective.

Myth #1: Entrepreneurs are born, not made.

It is true that entrepreneurs often have a flair for the creative and a lot of energy. However, just having these characteristics certainly does not turn you into an entrepreneur.

These talents by themselves are like unformed clay or an unpainted canvas. A true entrepreneur uses these characteristics and gathers the right skills, experience, and contacts. He or she constantly is trying to make improvements in his or her work and in him- or herself. You quite likely will find an entrepreneur in the "self help" aisle of a bookstore.

Though you are born with some of these characteristics, you can become an entrepreneur through discipline, desire, and commitment.

Myth #2: Anyone can start a business.

Although it is true that anyone can acquire a business license and open shop, there is far more to "starting a business" than starting up. The easiest part is starting up. The hardest part is surviving, sustaining, and building. It takes work to overcome, to build, to persevere, to create, and to succeed. Being a champion takes focus, creativity, diligence, time, and resources.

Anyone can start *up* a business, but not anyone can keep a business *open*. However, you **can** succeed if you use the right resources and are dedicated and committed.

Myth #3: Entrepreneurs are their own bosses and completely independent.

The dream of being "your own boss" can capture the attention of those working for someone else. There is this notion that the boss makes up the rules and those rules always benefit the boss. This is far from true.

Entrepreneurs, though independent, have to serve many masters, including customers, employees, families, and those involved in social and community obligations. Entrepreneurs, however, can make choices of whether they care to respond, when they care to respond, and what they care to respond to.

Eight Entrepreneurial Characteristics

Remember that entrepreneurs are striving to improve themselves. Therefore, if you want to be an entrepreneur and you are willing to work on it, you eventually can be one.

Over the years, people have studied entrepreneurs to determine what makes them successful. Certain characteristics show up repeatedly. Here are the eight characteristics that you will want to have and improve upon if you wish to be a successful entrepreneur:

1. Leadership
2. High energy
3. Self-confidence
4. Organization
5. Competitiveness
6. Preparation to work hard
7. The will to take risks
8. Communication skills

For redesign or home staging, you also will need creativity. The biggest value you can offer a client is to do something for her home that she would not have thought of herself because she simply cannot picture it in her mind. This career is not about hanging goldfish bowls from the ceiling. It is about helping your client do something that, no matter what she read or what she saw in a magazine, she could not do on her own.

Take a good, hard look at the list. You must have all these qualities to be a successful entrepreneur. Luckily, the items on the list are learnable. If you want to be an entrepreneur, be honest with yourself and then get to work.

Entrepreneurial Skills Assessment

Before launching any business on your own, you need to take a good hard look at yourself.

Consider the following assessment and check off the skills that apply to you.

Creativity

_____ I continually generate new ideas.

_____ I can improvise on the spur of the moment.

_____ I am willing to experiment with a new approach.

_____ I can visualize shapes, colors, and their relationship to each other.

Personality

_____ I am self-motivated and can manage my own time.

_____ I do not mind working alone for long stretches of time.

_____ My feelings are not easily hurt.

_____ I have drive, patience, determination, and a positive attitude.

Entrepreneurial

_____ I enjoy creative problem solving.

_____ I understand that there is more to my business than my service.

_____ I know that failure is a step in the process to success.

_____ I learn from my mistakes.

Entrepreneurial Skills Assessment

Organizational

_____ I am able to prioritize.

_____ I am good at record keeping.

_____ I have or can create a filing system.

_____ I can set and meet deadlines.

Customer Service

_____ I genuinely like people and care about the service I provide.

_____ I have the highest standard of honesty and integrity.

_____ I do not get frustrated easily.

Influencing/Persuading

_____ I can state my opinion without offending others.

_____ I can sell an idea to those making a decision.

_____ I can influence the attitudes of others.

_____ I can stimulate people to act.

Problem Solving

_____ I can see a problem as an opportunity.

_____ I gather facts before finding answers to problems.

_____ I can see the similarities and differences in problems I have solved.

_____ I can see many different solutions to a problem.

Support

_____ I have discussed my plans with my family and friends.

_____ My family and friends support my new business goal.

_____ I am in a good position financially to start my own business.

If you were able to check off the majority of these skills, or if you know that you can learn the skill or hire someone to handle it for you, you have the skills necessary to start and grow your new redesign or home staging business.

Five Entrepreneurial Resources

In addition to characteristics, entrepreneurs must have certain resources readily available:

1. **Enough money to see the project through:** Business ventures fail, due not to poor ideas but to lack of money. You will need to have a plan of action and know what startup money you need.

2. **Good health:** Being an entrepreneur requires long hours of hard work. Being in poor physical shape will not help you be successful in your new venture. Consider new habits like exercising, quitting smoking, or even taking a stress management class.

3. **Unique product or service:** Make sure that you are not selling what everyone else is selling already. Your service does not have to be brand new, but it should have a unique twist.

4. **Family/friend support:** Since being an entrepreneur takes a lot of time, you will want to have the support of family and friends. You will rely heavily on this support system. They will be who you turn to with your latest great idea and when hiring a recruit to help you move furniture.

5. **Experience:** You need to have an interest and at least some experience in your chosen field, even if it is not formal experience.

Just as with talents, these resources can be acquired. The real secret is knowing your strengths and weaknesses.

All these entrepreneurial skills fall into three main categories relating to the redesign or home staging business:

1. Personal relationships

2. Business practices

3. Creativity and design skills

Understanding relationships and having business savvy is more important than having creativity because, without business skills, your creative skills will go to waste. Though counterintuitive, it is true.

You Are Your Business

Some designers, consultants, and other independent professionals have all the business they need, while others struggle to get by, only to eventually lose heart and close up shop. The first thing to understand is that, in a service-oriented business such as design, you are the business. When people call you on the phone, they do not want to have their room redesigned. They want *you* to redesign their room. Any designer can make their room beautiful. It is up to you to create a relationship with them so they will hire you instead of your competitors.

Although pricing (see Chapter 2), naming your business, and putting together the right business plan is important (see Chapter 3 and Appendix 23), nothing is as important as the relationships you will establish.

In the end, you can name your business whatever you choose. It will not really matter because the client will deal with you and not with your name. He or she will be dealing with the choices you make in creating your business and then the choices you make when working with the public.

The personal relationship you establish with your client is essential, since working with someone in his or her own home is personal. As you begin a project to redesign and redecorate for a client, it is important that you determine how the client lives in his or her home.

Your client's habits will determine how you redesign a room. For instance, if your client works late at night in her lower-level living room, draperies offering privacy will be necessary. Learning that your client prefers to be barefoot will help you determine what kind of flooring would be best.

Before your project is complete, you may know your client's most private habits better than even her best friends do. Due to this intimate knowledge, you will become not only a designer but also a confidante and a friend.

Learning your client's needs and wants are paramount to having a good business relationship and, thus, a thriving business.

Money Matters

One of the greatest advantages of starting a redesign or home staging business is that operating it from your own home is possible. More than 90 percent of all redesigners start their business with no storefront, and the majority of these choose to remain a home business. Doing so keeps overhead low and may allow you to take a home business deduction on your taxes. Keep in mind that, if you start as a sole proprietorship, as many home design business owners do, you will have paperwork requirements when it comes to filing taxes.

••⌘••
Mary's Trade Tips

There are many talented and creative designers in this field who struggle to get by because they do not have the skills needed to run a business. You do not need to be the best designer to be successful — you need to be able to run the business. Therefore, it is imperative that you take the time to learn the business end of redesign and real estate staging and then use what you have learned.

Even with the low overhead, however, your goal in business is to make money. Although designing and creativity may be your passion, your business skills will determine your success.

You have to make money so you can stay in business. Some people are service-oriented and creative but cannot make the necessary shift to business, which is why it is necessary to develop these skills.

Business skills are those that help you make marketing decisions, create accurate client files, and return phone calls. These skills allow you to make a profit. If you want to stay in business, making a profit is not an option — it is a necessity.

Time for Creativity

Only after you have created a business persona and have your business processes in order are you ready to begin talking about creativity. Based on the popularity of HGTV, people are interested in home improvement and home design. They may believe they can improve their home by watching HGTV or by reading a book on the subject and then grabbing a paintbrush and rearranging their furniture, only to realize that it is not as easy as it looks. The fact is, many people do not have the time, talent, or inclination to undertake redesign projects or home staging themselves.

This means there are plenty of opportunities for entrepreneurs like you to start your business and offer your services. This is where your creativity comes into play.

In the redesign, redecorate, and home staging business, you will take stock of a person's furnishings and accessories and then rearrange them in the same space. For redesign, the purpose is to make the room the best it can be for the life style and enjoyment of the family. For home staging, the purpose is to make the room appealing to the broadest audience so that it can sell quickly and for more money. Regardless, as a redesigner or stager, you are going to have to use your creative skills.

It will be your sense of balance, eye for color, and attention to the details that will round out your ability to market your business. How you use your creativity is what will set your services apart from others.

Now that you know you need personal skills, business sense, and creativity, let us look at how you can get started.

Getting Your Feet Wet

You have taken a good, hard look at your wants and your skills, and you have decided that you have the personality, the talent, and the desire to run your own redesign or real estate staging business. So how do you get a little bit of real-world experience to make sure this is absolutely for you?

Hire a Redesigner

The easiest way to gain insight into the mechanics of a redesign or real estate staging business is to hire this service for your own home. In this way, you can shop the competition in the fullest sense. Doing so will allow you to view how someone else is doing the work.

Before you call someone, check out all the competition in your area by looking at Web sites. Then start calling around. Whoever ends up redesigning your home may turn into your mentor. Be sure to start developing your business relationships the moment you make your first call.

When you make the call, start out by being a typical customer and asking the following questions:

- How long will it take?
- Do you use any help?
- Can I work with you?
- How do you determine what to use?
- What do you charge?
- What if I need items I do not have?

Listen to how they answer the phone. Note how quickly they return your call. Listen to what they say. Note the things they said that made you feel comfortable. More important, note the things that were said that made you feel uncomfortable. Doing so will be invaluable.

Once you have decided on a redesigner for your own home, it is best to be upfront about what you are doing. Tell her that you love the HGTV shows. Tell her you are considering starting a business and you would like to hire her to come into your home. Then ask if she is comfortable with that. Some will be comfortable, and some will not. If they are not, do not be discouraged. Get on the phone and try someone else.

When you have someone willing to redesign your home, you will want to take copious notes. In addition to noting her telephone scripts, you will want to learn about:

- Pricing

- Services

- The process

You also will want to pay attention to the questions she asks you and get copies of the forms she uses. Finally, you will want to stay and watch what she does and take notes during that time as well.

Become an Intern

Another idea is to contact local firms and offer your services as an intern. Once again, you need to be upfront and tell them you are considering starting your own business. They may not share the behind-the-scenes aspect of their business with you, but they may be willing to use you on big projects in which they need an assistant to help them redecorate a room.

Gain Other Experience

Finally, you may consider getting experience through related design opportunities, such as the following:

- Home, furniture, and accessory stores

- Real estate agents

- Associated stores — plumbing fixtures, kitchen, and bath

- Architects

No matter how you go about gaining knowledge on the subject of redesign, you must remember that learning and education are a continual process.

Education, Reading, and More

Nothing beats experience, but when you do not have experience, using the experience of others is a great way to fill that gap. Reading this book is a great start. Even if you already have your business started, additional training through reading, conferences, or classes is a good idea. Doing so will keep you up to date on the latest trends in your own business, which keeps your business ahead of the competition. See Appendix 21 for more great books.

This is especially true in redesign. Interior decorating in the home changes every three to five years. In the 1950s the rule of thumb was to create a line around the room when hanging art. In the 1980s, country blue and peach were the "in" colors. Neither one of these is true now. Not only do you have to change business practices to keep up with the times; you also have to keep up concerning the decorating you do.

The characteristics of an entrepreneur coupled with the characteristics of a good decorator are many. The ability to juggle your duties as a logical businessperson and creative redesigner are crucial to your success. No one will have all the skills in the beginning — becoming a redesigner, redecorator, and home stager takes time and is an ongoing process.

Now that you know what it takes to become successful, it is time to look at what you have to offer your clients.

Chapter 2

What You Have to Offer

Who You Are and What You Do

Redesign, in its purest form, is simply using the furniture and accessories that a client has in his or her home and rearranging them to make the room look the best it can be. You add nothing. You do not shop. You do not make suggestions. You just rework the furniture, wall hangings, area rugs, and accessories.

Real estate staging can be as simple as an evaluation that leaves a homeowner with a list of things to do or renting furniture for a seller's empty home. The objective: to help the homeowner sell the home quickly and for maximum dollar value.

As a business owner, you have to determine if you want to be a purist or if you will add on other services. There is no right or wrong answer. It depends only on how you want your business to grow.

Why Add Services

There are two big reasons to add services beyond redesign or home staging. One reason is to give yourself variety in your work. Shopping for a client or adding window treatments to his or her home adds a dimension to your business that allows you to use your designing skills even further. The second reason will add to your bottom line. Once a client has worked with you, he or she will want to continue working with you. Offering more services will allow you to continue working with loyal clients.

You can determine what you ultimately want to do in your business by offering different services to your clients to see what you like to do and to see what they want you to do for them.

In the beginning, each client will be a learning experience. You will learn about yourself, your business, and what will bring in new clients. Try not to take mistakes you make personally. Every failure is a step to success. These experiences can teach you many things — how you work with people, how to communicate with clients, and how to establish your pricing. These early clients will prepare you for larger clients as your business grows.

Add-ons to Consider

There is no limit to the number of services you can offer your clients. If you have the knowledge and the time, and if the service relates in any way to design, you can turn that into an "add on" service.

Ask the Expert

Q. When you were deciding what services to offer in your business, what is one service you offered that you no longer offer?

A. Clients say they want a design plan for their home so they can turn their home into something beautiful on their own. The problem is that they cannot turn the plan into reality. If they had that talent, they would not have needed to call me in the first place. Then they are disappointed because the plan did not translate into the room of their dreams. Everyone ends up disappointed.

I no longer develop design plans for clients. It is my job to educate my clients and to help them understand how they can benefit from working with me so that everyone is satisfied with the outcome of the room.

Add-on services are those that go beyond a consultation and pure redesign. They include:

Personal shopping: After a redesign, you likely will find items, such as lighting, lacking. Therefore, you can choose to shop for your clients after a redesign to purchase items that would make their room look even better.

Patio or porch redesign: This is a great springtime redesign project. There is no reason a redesigner has to stay within the walls of a home.

Holiday and party decorating: People love to entertain during the holidays but may not have enough time to decorate. This service works well for the busy professionals on your client list.

Move-in services: This service can range from helping a new owner of a home decorate after he or she has unloaded boxes to being there as the movers arrive and putting everything in its place before the client ever arrives.

Custom window treatments: Window treatments may be missing or do not contribute to the look of your client's home, especially after a beautiful redesign. You can help your client by offering custom window treatments. You also can work with retail curtains in a way that turns something inexpensive into something that has a more custom look.

Full-service interior design: Once a redesign project is finished, your client may decide that new furnishings, paint, flooring, and even something as dramatic as new window sizes should change. To be involved in this kind of add-on, you may need an interior design license. You also will need to have good subcontractors in place.

Color consultations: Once you have redesigned a home, your client may want to purchase new furnishings or add color to the walls. Use your expertise to do a color consultation.

•◆⌘◆•
Mary's Trade Tips

Consider using a project fee for a color consultation, rather than charging by the hour. The value you bring is in introducing a beautiful color palette to the home. Just because you can do this quickly does not mean it has less value. Set a project fee for color consultations, such as $125 for up to four colors or $200 for five to nine colors. Be sure to research the going rate in your area.

Classes: Students are the best clients. They have seen you in action and have seen you at your best. As they go home and try to do the things you taught them, they may realize they need your help. Class attendees also may determine that they will not be able to do what you have taught them to do. Classes establish you as an expert.

Home transitions: This includes clients moving from a big house to a small house or a small house to a big house. This service also can include helping elderly clients move into a retirement community or an assisted living center.

Children's rooms: What a child wants at the age of four, five, or six is not what he wants when he turns 13. What he wants at 13 is not what he wants at 16. This leads to several changes before a child moves from home. Parents may not want to handle all these changes, especially if they have more than one child.

Organizing services: According to a new report entitled "Garage and Storage Shed Trends in the U.S." by the market research firm SBI, the 2006 market for storage products was more than $1.5 billion. This trend shows that America has a lot of things that need to be organized, so why not help?

Painting: Painting a room gives your client a new look quickly and easily. This service works really well for home stagers since it can give the home a new, fresh, clean look.

Faux finishing/furniture refinishing: By refinishing your client's furnishings, you will be able to turn the items into something that fits the newly redesigned room. Be sure that you learn these techniques from a professional before trying them with a client.

Virtual redesign: Different computer programs exist that can create a virtual room based on digital photographs. To offer virtual redesign, simply ask the client to send you eight to ten quality digital photographs, room dimensions, and window measurements. The most popular virtual redesign functions are wall color selection, custom window treatment ideas, and virtual furniture arrangements.

Interiorscaping: Professional interiorscapers consult with homeowners to create indoor gardens that complement home design and the personal tastes of the owners. These indoor-garden experts then install the gardens.

In home staging, you can move beyond a consultation and use what you know about redesign to help the client achieve his or her ultimate goal — selling the home. You pack objects, declutter rooms, rearrange furniture and accessories, and give the home curb appeal in this hands-on process. You may go so far as to rent or purchase furniture or accessories for the client.

You can be extremely successful in home staging using any of these approaches. It is simply a decision you have to make. There is no right or wrong way. What is right or wrong is how you go about doing it.

It would be wrong to rent a warehouse full of furniture if you do not have a marketing plan that will help you get that furniture into homes. It also would be wrong to have a warehouse of furniture in a location that will not support a full-service home staging business.

Add-ons open up a completely new avenue for your business. There is no need to limit yourself to those listed here. Look for niches needed by potential clients in your area and that correspond to your talents.

Ask the Expert

Q. Why would I want to do a redesign before a full interior design? It sounds like a waste of my time and my client's time.

A. Even though I am a full-service design firm, virtually every project I do for a client begins with a room redesign. It is not that much more of an investment for the client, and in the end he or she saves money.

Clients cannot visualize a room. They may think that they need all new furniture in order for a room to look good, when what they really need is proper placement. By beginning with a redesign, they will learn what pieces of furniture to get rid of and those that are perfect. The redesign will show us what gaps need to be filled to make the room the best it can be.

Another thing that happens is a client thinks that new furniture magically will make a room look better. Say she has an old, ugly sofa, old accent pieces, and new accessories – and let's also say they are all in the wrong place. So not only is the furniture old, but the room does not feel good. In her mind, she thinks a new sofa will make the room great, but the room will be exactly the same, only with a bright, shiny new sofa. It is not that she does not need a new sofa. Where you put that new sofa is critical to the feel of the room.

The approach I use is to redesign first with the things my client has. I know that the room is going to have a sofa, so I put my client's sofa in the right place. She may have the ugliest lamp on Earth, and I know that we are not going to use it, but I will use it as a placeholder for the new lamp. This makes it easier to visualize the room and see what new items are needed.

Clients are uncomfortable with the interior design process because they cannot tell if the floor plans you have drawn are going to look good in real life. Marking down all the furnishings as little boxes on a piece of paper is not easy to visualize, especially if your client has not worked with floor plans before. Redesign alleviates this pressure because clients can see a sofa in the right place and will understand that a lovely new sofa in that spot will be just right.

You Are Worth It

In almost any new business activity, the issue of "what should I charge?" must be addressed. After all, it is a question that comes up in every sales transaction. By developing your pricing structure and sticking to it, you will succeed.

Cost and Price: How Are They Related?

Pricing should be determined with a clear distinction between cost and value. Cost and price are related but only in this way: If the price does not recover your costs, you will not be in business long.

Because of this one critical price-cost relationship, it is important to know the true cost of a product or service. More businesses fail initially because their prices are too low rather than too high.

The Most Important Element of Pricing: Value

The most important element of pricing is understanding the value of what you are selling. The value is measured by the benefit of the service against what the service costs your client.

People struggle with the concept of value. When you have a natural skill that comes easily, you may feel it must not be worth much. This translates into business failure. If you do not charge appropriately for your services, you may wear yourself out or, worse, become resentful of your work. This will lead you to leave the business, and then you will no longer be using your design skills to bring a valuable service to others.

You do not need to feel badly about making money. You work hard. You use your knowledge, your skills, and your design sense. It may come easily to you, but that does not mean it should be free.

If everyone could do it, they would not need you. The truth is that not everyone can do it and not everyone who can wants to. That is why people need you. If they need your services, they will be willing to pay for them.

Remember that the service you are bringing is worth something to other people. They hire you because they want what you have to offer.

What About Freebies?

New redesigners and home stagers are known to give away services when they first get started as a way of getting themselves in front of potential clients. This is known as the numbers game — the more jobs you have, even if you make no money, the more likely you are to succeed.

This is a debatable strategy. Giving your services away free can give your client the idea that your services are of no value. This is not true. What you know can make a world of difference.

If you do a redesign consultation for free, you are going to give the client many tips and ideas. For instance, moving a picture down six inches will give the room a focal point. Or moving the curtains up six inches will make your room feel taller. These a are worth something. If used, they will change the way the room looks. If a client can get that information for free, he has no incentive to purchase it from you. He will see how wonderful you are, but it was free so he will not see the value.

If you are a home stager and have done a free staging job for a real estate agent, another agent may see you and decide to pay you. However, the first agent is unlikely to ever buy your services. Once again, you gave away the service for free, leaving your expertise valueless.

••✦⌘✦••

Mary's Trade Tips

If you feel strongly that you need to do some work for free to gain exposure for your business, be sure you gain that exposure. Request that your client brings in five friends before you do the project, and then have the five friends be at the home with you when the homeowner sees the fabulous work you do. Then you can offer those five people a "special introductory" rate if, when you do their work, they bring in five friends. This targets your efforts and guarantees someone will be talking about your work.

You Are Worth What You Charge

When you are pricing your services, it is important that you find out what others around you are charging. You need to know what is working in your area.

Be sure to use this only as a starting point and not as the right figure for you. If everyone is charging $75 an hour, you should not charge the same amount. You will just become another face in the crowd. It is better to be in the higher range than in the lower range.

If you do not know how to differentiate yourself, the easiest way is by price. People put value on money. If you are free, you must not be that valuable. If you are more expensive than everyone else, you must be valuable.

••✦⌘✦••

Mary's Trade Tips

You can change more, but be sure you have the talent to back it up.

Project Pricing Versus Hourly Pricing

If you are selling a service by the hour, you need to take into account the actual billable hours available. Billable hour estimates range from 1,000 to 1,500 hours per year. Once you have determined your estimated hourly rate, you can use it to decide if you will earn more than the average fast-food employee on a particular assignment. You can also use the rate to prepare project rates – a single all-inclusive fee when Project X is delivered for Y amount by Z deadline.

••✦⌘✦••

Mary's Trade Tips

Some real estate stagers charge by the square foot. This may be a way to determine price if you are installing wallpaper or painting, but it is not a good practice for staging. A 3,500 square foot home could be in need of just the basic recommendations, while a 900 square foot home could be in need of every trick in the book. Evaluate the space before quoting a price.

Avoid This Business Blunder

In the beginning, many designers start with an hourly fee because they are comfortable with the theory. I would propose that you do not do it. Why be like everyone else? Do not even talk about time. Talk about what you can do and what it can do for your client. Talk about the value redesign can bring to their home. Explain how redesign eliminates the stress of decision-making. Once you talk to them at a value level, price is no longer a problem.

With hourly rates, you are limited by the hours in a day. Project pricing is not limited by time; it is only limited by the value your client receives. For this reason you may want to consider using project pricing.

••✦⌘✦••
_____

Mary's Trade Tips

You need to revisit your price structure regularly. One year from now you will be far more experienced and should be charging a higher price.

_____

Are You Priced Right?

People will tell you when you are overpriced. No one will tell you when you are under-priced. You know you are under-priced when everybody you talk to can afford you. Unless you are planning to work extreme volume, not every person should be able to afford you. You need to remember that you are not a big box discount store.

If five people call and like what you do, and every one of them says there is no way they are going to pay your fee, you may need to lower your prices. However, if every person who calls jumps at your services, your prices are probably too low.

Ask the Expert

Q. I worry that I will quote my client a fee and it will not take me long to complete the project. I do not want to cheat him. What should I do?

A. It is not cheating the client when you deliver what is expected. I do not tell my clients how many hours I will spend on a task. I tell them how much they need to invest with me to achieve their goal.

Ask the Expert

For example, let us say my client wants me to shop for accessories for her home. I will tell her that it will be X number of dollars for me to shop, bring in the objects I found, and have her review them. In this way, nobody has to think about how long you are going to take to get the task done. The client does not worry about how long you are gone or how long you are shopping. Time is not a factor.

If I walk into the first store and find everything my client needs, I do not feel as if I cheated my client. I am being paid for my expertise. Because of my expertise, I can see the needed pieces in that store. If I were not an expert, I might miss what is there and have to go to several more stores. On the other hand, if I go into 18 stores before I find the right items, my clients still get the same price.

They are paying me to achieve the goal. The price you quoted, which is the price they accepted, is worth it to them. In the end, they want a goal achieved, and they are willing to pay the money to achieve that goal.

Your clients will look to you to provide them with the services they need. When a client first calls you, she will understand only that she needs something done to her home. It is up to you to determine what services you will offer and how your services can meet her needs.

With need comes cost, and your clients expect you to charge for your services. Despite a desire to avoid the money question, you must address it before ever talking with your first client. This will make everyone more comfortable with the transaction.

The next item on your "begin your business to-do list" will help you discover what you need to do to deliver these services.

Chapter 3

A Plan to Succeed

Getting your business thoughts down on paper is key to your success. This plan — this business plan — will help keep your goals in focus and guide you as your business grows. It is also necessary to help you get financing if you need money from a lender to get your business off the ground.

Keep in mind, however, that one of the pros for starting a redesign, redecorating, and real estate staging business is that you can get started with little expense, using equipment you already own.

Since this is the case, let us first look at a simplified plan that will help you as your grow your business.

A Simplified Business Plan

The best way to write a simplified business plan is to examine and answer the following questions:

- What?

- Who?

- Where?

- How?

- Goals?

To answer the "what" question, you need to understand what your business is and what it does. Your answer might look like the following:

I am going to provide the services of redesign. Redesign entails working with a client's own items and accessories so that the room can look its most beautiful. My redesign business also will include shopping, window treatments, and color consultations.

Or

I am going to work with realtors and homeowners to help them stage their home so they can have the best space for sale. To do this, I will rework what the client already owns. I will rent furniture and accessories as needed.

The "who" question can be a bit tough in the beginning. When you first start out, the answer will be the people you already know. Let these people know what you are doing. If you have been dabbling in design already, hopefully some of these people will need you to do work for them.

It is the same for home staging. Everyone knows someone with a home on the market. Find out who that person is and talk to him.

Your "who" will develop beyond friends and people you know. Once this happens, you will need to be more specific. It then will be time to answer this question: "Who is my favorite client?"

The answer should not be, "Anyone who wants to pay me." This is too broad. Instead, think about the clients you have worked with already. Think about the jobs that appealed to you most and why they appealed to you.

You might find that you really enjoy working with mothers with small children because you like making their homes beautiful as well as safe for their children. You might enjoy working with businesswomen who do not have the time to redesign on their own but wish to have a beautiful home.

In the beginning, your "who" is truly anyone. However, your marketing should be geared toward your perfect client. Getting specific about whom you are talking to helps you market effectively.

• ◆ ⌘ ◆ •

Mary's Trade Tips

Although anybody can be your customer, you need to find your niche. Once you know whom you want to work with, it is your job to educate those that you are targeting as to what you do and why they need you.

"Where" is an easy question to answer. You are only limited by how far you want to drive. The best place to start is in your own neighborhood.

"How" will you get started? In the beginning, you do not need a lot. The list in Appendix 4 is a helpful guideline, but you will not need all those items for your first job. The business equipment needed is likely already in your home. You need a computer, a printer, a phone, and files that you can access. Realistically, you can get started with as little as $500.

Other "hows" include:

- Having the skills

- Learning the steps outlined in this book

- Researching how other people make it happen

Finally, you have the "goals" question. What do you want to achieve, and how will you achieve this? Set a goal for the near future so that you have something to work toward. After time has passed, you can tweak it to reflect your situation more accurately.

Such goals might include:

- In six months, I would like to hire someone to do the administrative work.

- I would like to do one design job a week.

- I would like to earn X dollars per year.

Your goal may be to do a certain number of jobs per week. To determine what number is realistic, you have to look at how long a typical room redesign takes you to complete. If it takes you all day and you can only work four days a week, at most, you will be able to do four jobs a week. Of course, if the job really takes you all day, you will be exhausted before you complete four in a week. This means that you really can complete only two or three.

If you have two jobs a week at $500 a job, that will bring in $1,000 a week.

•◆⌘◆•
Mary's Trade Tips

As you start your new business, you will want to ask your first clients to help you obtain new clients. Ask the client who she knows that is just like her. Since people hang out with others who are similar, she should have some ideas of friends who may need your service. Ask for their contact information. Better yet, ask her to allow you to do a design presentation in her home for a whole group of friends.

You also can work in reverse, stating that you want $50,000 per year in income.

No matter which way you word your goal, you must look at what you currently are doing and what you need to do to make the goal happen.

Ask the Expert

Q. How do I know what kind of goals to create if I have never been in business before?

A. Here are four questions you can ask to create realistic goals that will grow your business:

1. How much business do I have now?

You can answer this as the number of active clients or the amount of money you make a week. No matter how you answer this question, you have to quantify it.

2. How much business do I really want?

You cannot say "a lot." If you have three clients and you want to have five, you need to determine how to get two more. You might have to quantify it

Ask the Expert

even more if you want five clients monthly. Just because you have five today does not mean you have five clients four weeks from now.

3. What is my 90-day goal?

If you have two clients and you want five, then in the next 90 days, you want to get three new clients. You need to know every day what your goal is. Knowing your goal will determine what you do during your day.

4. What am I going to do when I reach my goal?

This is the reward part of goal setting. Your reward should be something that encourages you to want to meet your goals. Personally, I like my reward to have nothing to do with work because I work all week.

SMART Goals

As you write your goals, you need to have a way to evaluate those goals. A good way to evaluate your goals is to determine if they are SMART goals:

S = Specific

M = Measurable

A = Attainable

R = Realistic

T = Timely

Specific: Goals should be straightforward and emphasize what you want to happen. Specifics help you focus your efforts and clearly define what you are going to do. If you have a specific goal, you will be more likely to attain that goal. To set a specific goal you must answer the six "W" questions:

- Who: Who is involved?

- What: What do I want to accomplish?

- Where: Identify a location.

- When: Establish a time frame.

- Which: Identify requirements and constraints.

- Why: Determine specific reasons, purpose, or benefits of accomplishing the goal.

A general goal would be "My business will make money." But a specific goal would be "My business will make $50,000 per year."

Measurable: If your goal is not measurable, it is probably not manageable either. Establish a specific way to measure your progress toward your goal. Measuring a goal helps you stay on track and meet your deadline.

To determine if your goal is measurable, ask questions such as "How much?" "How many?" and "How will I know when it is accomplished?"

Attainable: If a goal is important to you, you will find as many ways as possible to achieve that goal.

Realistic: This is not a synonym for "easy." Realistic, in this case, means "do-able." To be realistic, a goal must represent an objective that you want to work toward and that you can work toward. A goal can be both high and realistic; you are the only one who can decide just how high your goal should be. Be sure that every goal represents substantial progress.

Your goal is realistic if you truly believe that it can be accomplished.

Another way to know if your goal is realistic is to determine if you have accomplished anything similar in the past or ask yourself what conditions would have to exist to accomplish this goal.

Timely: A goal should be grounded within a time frame. With no time frame tied to it, there is no sense of urgency. If you want to have five active clients, by when do you want to have them? "Someday" will not work. If you do not set a time, the commitment is too vague. It tends not to happen because you feel you can start at any time. Without a time limit, there is no urgency to start taking action now.

You will benefit from goals and objectives if they are SMART.

••⌘••

Mary's Trade Tips

This business is great for someone who does not need to make a living at it. A good redesigner can make extra money by relying solely on word of mouth. You can build your own personal network, especially if you have lived forever in your neighborhood and have been involved in all the local activities and clubs, such as the PTA and scouts.

Those who have seen your beautiful home know what you can do, and you just have to state that you now are doing this type of work as a business. Your contacts invite you over, and you do a redesign for them.

This is more like a hobby with low overhead and decent pay. You are not paying for advertising. You are not paying for any marketing. You can launch yourself with less than $500.

If you want to grow your business to an income of six digits, you have to be in the business of marketing. If you want to be a big business, you have to do big business. If you want to be a decorator with a bit of spare money, this simple model works.

Choosing a Name

One of the exciting decisions you will make before opening your doors is naming your redesign, redecorating, and real estate staging business. The name of your business is the "first impression" a prospective client will have of you.

Here are six tips for determining a good name for your business:

1. **Is it memorable?** A business name is one of the first things a person learns about a business. When clients walk away, you want them to remember the name and desire the service.

2. **Can nine out of ten people spell it?** This is important. If they cannot spell your business name, they will not be able to find you in the phone book or on the Internet. How can you determine if you have an easy-to-spell name? Take a survey. Tell people your name and ask them to spell it. If nine people can spell it for every ten people you ask, you have a winner. If not, you need to rethink your name.

3. **What image does it create for others?** Ask people this question, "When I say the name, what do you think of?" If they have the right idea, it is a good name. Rethink the name if they come up with something totally different. You might think your name is cute and catchy, but it may confuse others. If your business name does not convey the work that you perform, you may miss out on prospective clients.

4. **Is the domain name available?** If you are going to be Mary Larsen Designs, having **www.MaryLarsenDesigns .com** is important. You can go to **www.godaddy**

.com to find out if the domain name you want is still available.

5. **Does it represent all you do now and all you plan to do in the future?** When you name your business you want the name to mean something to the person who hears it, without creating a name that is too limiting. For example, you may not want to be "Jane Smith Real Estate Staging" if you think you may one day add other services to your business.

6. **Small-business owners can use their own names for their business.** For example, if your name is Jane Smith, you may consider "Jane Smith Redesign." Your personal name should not be the first choice if your name is unusual or cannot be spelled. If your last name is Riemenschneider, you certainly would not want to use Riemenschneider's Redesign. No one will ever find you. It would be far better to have something like Rainbow Redesign that people can spell.

Plan for the Unexpected

Having a plan means you know the general direction in which you want your business to grow. Having a plan, however, should not limit you. Your plan was created by you and can be changed by you. If you see a new niche or determine you like working with a new type of client, change your plan to accommodate these new desires.

Also realize that emergencies happen and your plan may not have that particular emergency contingency. Although a plan is necessary in business, being able to handle the unexpected is also necessary. In unusual situations, throw out your plan for 24 to 48 hours and then go back to the plan when the emergency is over.

> ### *Avoid This Business Blunder*
>
> My schedule does not allow someone to call me and ask me to do an emergency project. However, there are times that saying yes to an emergency is just the right thing to do.
>
> HGTV's *Extreme Makeover* called and asked me to help on a local home – in two days. I was able to adjust my schedule and go. I called clients and asked to reschedule their projects, and they were thrilled that their designer was going to be on Extreme Makeover!
>
> Others were asked to participate. Some did not want to be flexible – they did not want this project to interfere with their written plan.
>
> Being part of HGTV's *Extreme Makeover* show was not part of my plan, but it was an incredible experience, and it has created many opportunities I would not previously have had.
>
> The moral of the story is that you should be prepared to be flexible.

A simple business plan is all you will need when opening your redesign, redecorating, and real estate staging business. It may be all you ever need unless you add a partner or seek financial assistance through a bank or an investor. Completing a formal business plan is simply an extension of the one here. A formal business plan template and questions to ask to create this template are in Appendix 23.

The formalities are out of the way. The next step is creating a legal entity, setting up your office, and creating business administration processes.

Chapter 4

Setting Up Shop

Home Sweet Home

A redesign, redecorating, and real estate staging business is perfectly suited for a home office. This business does not require a storefront since you give consultations in a client's home and do all the hands-on work there as well. Those jobs you do at home, such as choosing color palettes or creating custom window treatments, do not need a storefront.

The advantages of working from home are numerous:

- Low startup cost
- Flexible work hours

- Low overhead cost
- No commuting costs
- Lower wardrobe expenses
- Tax deduction on office portion of your home

Disadvantages include:

- Small or confining work space
- No peer group for interaction
- Limited support group
- Sole responsibility for your workday
- Managing your work versus personal tasks
- Managing family expectations

Creating a personal workspace, joining a local professional group, and learning to manage your day can reduce the disadvantages of working at home.

Behind Closed Doors

Your ideal home office is a room of its own with a door you can shut at the end of the workday. This will help you maintain balance between your work and your life. Other options include setting up a distinct space in your home separated from the living space with a folding screen or a drapery. Even placing an armoire in the living room that can house your computer and files and be closed at the end of the day can work as your office.

Another reason for a dedicated office space is to help your family know which role you currently are playing. When you are in your designated office space, you are a redesigner. When you are in the other areas of your home, you are a spouse and a parent.

Make Contact

People working in large offices have daily peer interaction. This interaction provides friendship and education on the issues concerning the business. As a small-business owner working out of the home, you will not find this kind of interaction. Therefore, you need to seek it elsewhere.

You can do this by joining a professional group that has local meetings. This is not to say that you cannot join a national organization, but your business will grow as you meet those in your area, so start on the local level.

Try the Interior Design Society, the Window Coverings Association of America, or something like the Chamber of Commerce if you cannot find a design-specific organization. You will be so grateful for the wealth of information you find there.

Managing Your Solo Day

When you are on your own at home, you have many roles to play. These roles may include:

- Decision maker
- Marketer
- Bookkeeper
- Sales force
- Secretary
- Computer guru
- Public relations expert

Let us not forget what you do for a living:

- Redesigner
- Shopper
- Redecorator
- Seamstress
- Color expert
- Real estate home stager

What you have to do in a day can be daunting if you do not effectively manage your tasks. Here are three rules that can help:

1. **Put first things first.** Some tasks are always there and pressing, such as answering e-mails from support groups. Other tasks are important, such as contacting customers on a timely basis. It is up to you to separate the pressing from the important. Important tasks are those that advance you toward your goals.

2. **Use lists.** Whether it is on paper or on the computer, list everything you need to do. You then can prioritize the list and pull off the top priorities for your daily to-do list. Then, as you do them, cross off or delete completed items. There is something emotionally satisfying about seeing a list of items crossed off at the end of the day. This way, each day is manageable with nothing important lost in the process.

3. **Limit distractions.** Every time you stop what you are doing to check on another task, you waste time. For instance, if you are working on a color consultation report for a client and answer the phone every single time it rings, each interruption costs you a minimum of ten minutes. If you answer the phone four times in an hour, you have lost 40 minutes of work time. The solution is to turn off the ringer and let your voicemail answer the call.

Avoid This Business Blunder

My distraction used to be e-mail. E-mail is important because it is networking; however, there is a fine line between important and going too far. I realized that I was spending about 15 percent of my day on e-mail, yet none of that correspondence led to new clients or the growth of my business. This is when I knew that something was wrong.

Avoid This Business Blunder

Now I check my e-mail just twice a day. Doing so keeps the distractions to a minimum and allows me to spend time doing those things that grow my business.

Despite the things you become responsible for when you are on your own, remember that you are in charge. This means you decide what you do when. If you do not like the results, you can change your priorities.

Get It Done

Procrastination is a problem for nearly everyone at some point in time. Understanding how to overcome procrastination starts with understanding why you procrastinate in the first place.

One reason for procrastination is that the task is new and you do not know how to get started. If you have never written a press release, you may not know how to get started. Instead of writing the release, you find other things to do.

Perhaps you know how to do the task, but it scares you. For instance, you may know how to call potential customers, but the idea of selling your services to someone you have never met scares you.

The biggest reason for procrastination is that you do not like to do what needs to be done. For redesigners, this may be an administrative task, such as billing or answering e-mails.

The best remedy for this type of procrastination is recognizing the tasks you dislike doing and having the discipline to do them at the time of day you feel your best. If you are a morning person, do not do the fun, creative project first. Do the one horrible task and get it behind you. The rest of the day will be fabulous as you do what you love to do.

Eventually the growth of your business will allow you to hire someone to do those disliked tasks. However, even when this happens, there will always be items on your to-do list that you do not find appealing. Be disciplined and do them first.

••⌘••
Mary's Trade Tips

One problem you may have with procrastination is that you become caught up in tasks without recognizing those tasks as procrastination. You can work hard all week long, look back on the week, and realize that nothing you did brought you a new client or brought in a paycheck. A way to address this is to write everything down that you do for two to three days. When you check your e-mail, write down that task and write the number of minutes spent on the task. No matter what you do, write it down. Now look at how you are spending your time. Once you know how your time is spent, you can increase the time you spend on tasks that grow your business and cut down on tasks that have little value.

Keep It Separate, Keep It Legal

In order to take the tax write-offs available to a home-based business, you will need to keep your business files and home files completely separate. In addition to paperwork, you also will want to keep your office and home expenses separate. If the IRS audits you, having a separate business checking account will keep a tax audit carefully focused.

For example, if you are audited for your personal medical expenses and the IRS asks to see your checkbook, you may be in trouble if you commingled business and personal funds in that same account. Once your business records are in front of the auditor, the audit will now spread to issues unrelated to your health care deductions.

The cleaner your records, the easier an audit will be. If you write a $50 check for postage just before Christmas using your personal checking account, an auditor might question whether that check is truly a business expense or your own personal Christmas card postage expense. Writing a check for postage on your business account would not cause the same concerns.

The logical extension of that thought is to pay for every questionable, borderline expense from your business checking account so you could write it off. That is not a good idea for several reasons:

- It is unethical to take business deductions for personal expenses.

- It is illegal.

- There is no guarantee that the IRS will accept the business check you wrote to the office supply company for the pencils, notebook paper, and glue you bought in September for your children.

- You will not know exactly how much your business is earning and spending. This means you will be reducing your income artificially. Although this will reduce your income taxes now, it also will reduce your allowable retirement contributions, Social Security benefits, and chances for getting a business loan or home mortgage in the future.

Keep your business checking account clear of unrelated income as well. If you need to fund your business with cash from your personal account, always do it by depositing a check that you can show in an audit. If a relative gives you a financial gift for Christmas, deposit it in your personal account and then write a check to your business account. Otherwise, an auditor might view those deposits as undeclared income.

If you have a home office, pay shared expenses, like utility bills, out of your business account so that you do not lose track of any of them. At tax time, you will only be able to deduct a prorated share of those expenses, but you will have all of them on hand.

You absolutely, positively must keep your personal records and effects separate from your home office if you want to take the home-office deduction. This strict separation means that you should not keep your life insurance policy or your children's immunization records in your home office filing cabinet.

However, there is one situation that applies to redesigners in which you can combine personal and business use of your home without losing the home-office deduction. You are allowed to take deductions for space you use at home to store business inventory, such as paper supplies or laser toner, even if that space is shared, as long as it is your primary inventory storage space.

Another area in which you likely want to separate business and personal matters is your computer. The best answer to this is to have two computers. Give your old computer to your family for personal use and get a new computer that is strictly a business computer. If you do this, you will not have to keep a log of your computer time;

it will be assumed that it is strictly a business computer that is fully deductible or depreciable. Additionally, you will have a backup computer to use if your business computer dies.

If you only have one computer in the house, you will have to keep a log of your business and professional use in order to write off your business percentage. Nevertheless, beware. Provide a log that shows you used the computer in your home office 98 percent for business and 2 percent to do a database of your music collection, and you can lose your entire home-office deduction.

It is also a good idea to have a separate business credit card, for the same reasons as the business checking account. Doing so provides a clear record of business-related expenses. Some people prefer paying the extra fees for an American Express card for their businesses; it provides an extra set of receipts in the monthly statement so expense reports are easier to compile.

You also should consider having a gasoline card in your company name and have all fill-ups, maintenance, and repairs done on that card. People who use their cars for business can accumulate a higher level of deductible expenses if they track their real auto costs instead of just taking the 48.5-cents-per-mile deduction.

The Legal End of Business

Getting your business legally squared away is imperative to its operation and to your liability. Much of the legal information you need to start a redesign or staging business is located online.

Choosing a Legal Entity

Determining what legal form your business should take is one of the first questions you have to answer when starting your business. There is no right or wrong answer. The key is to understand the available options and determine what best fits your needs.

There are four main ways you can organize your business: sole proprietorship, partnership, corporation, and limited liability company. Each has its own set of advantages and disadvantages.

A sole proprietorship is a business that is owned directly by a single individual. That individual is solely responsible for all aspects of the business and is personally liable for all debts, even those in excess of the amount invested in the business. The advantages of a sole proprietorship include:

- Low organization costs

- Greatest freedom from regulation

- Possible tax advantages (taxation of owner at his/her individual rate, owner may deduct losses from his/her own individual return)

- Minimal working capital

The disadvantages include:

- Unlimited liability

- Difficulty in raising capital (must use own money or borrow)

A partnership is a business jointly owned by two or more individuals. Each of the individuals is personally liable for the debts of the partnership. In some respects, the law treats a partnership as a legal entity, but in others, it does not. The rights and privileges of the partners and the partnership are defined by law and the partnership agreement.

The advantages to a partnership are similar to those of a sole proprietorship. One additional benefit is that a partnership allows for additional capital and management resources since more than one person is contributing to the company. In addition to the disadvantages of a sole proprietorship, a partnership also raises the issue of divided authority.

A corporation is a separate legal entity that acts as a single person and is created under statutory law. The corporation owns the business and, in turn, issues shares of stock to individuals investing in the corporation.

The advantages of a corporation include:

- Limited liability (investors may be liable only for the amount invested)

- Ease of transferring ownership (selling shares)

- Ease of raising capital (selling shares)

- Possible tax advantage (corporate tax rate, shareholders taxed only on dividends received)

Although the advantages are great, so are the disadvantages. To be a corporation, your record keeping is more closely scrutinized. Laws for corporations are stricter and differ from state to state. Finally, financially, corporations are more expensive to organize and can have double taxation issues.

The last category is the limited liability company. When all requirements are fulfilled, a limited liability company (LLC) is taxed as a partnership, instead of a corporation, for federal tax purposes. However, in contrast to a partnership, an LLC may allow its owners to be involved in the management of the business without exposure to personal liability. An LLC allows you to have limited liability, reduced organizational costs, relaxed regulation, and flexible allocation of income/expenses.

You can do the research yourself to make determinations about the best way for you to organize your business. Talking with other small-business owners to gain insight from their experiences is highly recommended. These small-business owners also will be helpful in leading you to reputable bookkeepers, lawyers, or accountants, if you find yourself in need of those services.

Talking with a lawyer concerning your small-business entity is advisable.

State Registration

Once you have a name for your company, you will want to register that name in your state. Doing so will keep someone else from choosing and using the same name.

If you are going to do business under a name other than your personal name, you will need to check with your state's attorney general's office to see if you need to register. You can find these offices online. These sites provide a good deal of information concerning how to register for a name. If you need help finding this office, visit State and Local Government on the Internet at **www.statelocalgov.net**.

You also might want to trademark your name to protect it. You can trademark on a national or statewide level. To register your business as a local trademark, contact the secretary of state's office in your area. To register as a national trademark, you will need to contact the U.S. Patent and Trademark Office (**www.uspto.gov**).

There is also a search engine (Trademark Electronic Search System, or TESS) that can help you determine if the name has already been trademarked.

City Business License

Your city and your county likely require a permit to operate your business. To find out if a license is needed, you can search on the Internet using your county name and state. For example, search for "wake county, nc, local government," which then will direct you to the information needed for setting up your business.

You also can call your city or county's local government office, and someone there will be able to assist you. You might find that a license is not required.

Sales Tax

In a redesign and staging business, it is common to purchase items and resell them to your clients. If you do this, a sales tax will apply.

Sales tax rates and rules differ from state to state and city to city. According to the National Retail Federation, 45 states and 7,500 cities, counties, and jurisdictions impose sales taxes. States call these taxes by various names: sales tax, franchise tax, transaction privilege tax, use tax, and more. Some are the responsibility of the seller, and others are the buyer's responsibility.

If you are going to collect sales tax, you must get a license from your state. If your state does not require a business license, you will acquire a sales tax identification number. On each taxable transaction, you calculate the applicable sales tax, collect it from the buyer, keep tax records, and then file a tax return and pay the taxes to your state. You will pay monthly, quarterly, or annually, depending on your level of sales.

Many states exempt services such as redesign. Yet, even within a state, these rules can be inconsistent. Contact your state's Department of Revenue to find out how sales tax will affect you concerning your sales and services.

Getting an Employer Identification Number

As a business entity, you will need to apply for an Employer Identification Number (EIN). To do so, you need to prepare and submit an IRS form called the SS-4. Fortunately, you can fill out and submit an SS-4 online using the following URL: **https://sa1 .www4.irs.gov/sa_vign/newFormSS4.do.**

To complete the online SS-4 form or the paper SS-4 form, carefully follow these steps:

1. **Identify the legal name of your new company.** You enter the new, full legal name of your company into box 1.

2. **Identify the trade name if that name differs from the legal name.** As the form indicates, you enter the trade name of the business into box 2 if your trade name differs from the legal name.

3. **Provide the firm's address.** You enter the mailing address information into boxes 4a and 4b. If the business's street address differs from the mailing address, you also need to enter the street address into boxes 5a and 5b.

4. **Identify the county and state of the new business.** For example, if the county is Anycounty County, you enter Anycounty into the county box of box 6 and then enter your state into the state box.

5. **Identify yourself.** To do this, enter your full name into box 7a. Then, enter your Social Security number or individual taxpayer identification number, also referred to as an EIN, into box 7b.

6. **Identify the entity.** If you choose an LLC, in box 8a, mark the "Other" box and then specify "single member LLC" if the LLC has one owner.

7. **Explain why you need an EIN.** You mark one of the buttons in box 9 to indicate the reason you are requesting the EIN. For example, if you have just set up an LLC for a new business, you can mark the "Started New Business" button. You also might mark the "Other" business and then enter "LLC formation" into the blank provided. If you indicate you are starting a business, briefly describe the type of business using the space provided.

8. **Indicate when business activity started.** Using box 10 of the SS-4, indicate when your business started operating by choosing the month, day, and year from the drop-down list boxes.

9. **Identify the last month of the accounting year using box 11.** In most cases, an accounting year ends in December. This is what you will enter into box 11 unless you are selecting a month other than December.

10. **Indicate when you first paid or will first pay wages using the drop-down list boxes in box 12.** For example, if you first paid or will first pay wages on January 1, 2007, you enter JAN 1, and 2007.

11. **Use box 13 to indicate how many employees you plan to have.** Alternatively, if you do not expect to have employees, enter a 0 into the Agriculture, Household, and Other boxes.

12. **Describe (at least in a general way) the principal activity of your new business using box 14.** As a redesigner, none of the existing categories fits your new business. Therefore, mark the "other" button and add a short description to the field that follows the "other" button.

13. **Describe what you sell.** Use box 15 to describe the principal product or service provided.

14. **Indicate whether you previously have applied for an EIN.** You can do this by marking either the Yes or No box in box 16a. If you indicate that you have applied for an EIN before, fill in the blanks in box 16b with the old entity's legal and trade name. Then, if possible, use box 16c to specify when you previously applied for the EIN, the city and state where you applied, and the actual EIN.

15. **Submit the SS-4 form to the IRS.** If you are using the online version of the SS-4 form, you simply click the Next button to submit. The IRS server then validates the SS-4 form you have filled out.

If the IRS server finds an error, it re-displays the form with red messages describing the error. You need to fix the error and click the Next button again.

If the IRS server does not find any errors, it gives you a preliminary EIN number. Print the Web page that provides the EIN for your records. Additionally, scroll down the page to the hyperlink that says "click here to print a completed version of the SS-4 form." Following the on-screen instructions, print a copy of the completed SS-4 form.

If you have prepared a paper version of the SS-4 form, you mail or fax the completed form to the following address or fax number:

SS-4 Form Fax Information

Attn: EIN Operation
Philadelphia, PA 19255
Fax-TIN: 859-669-5760

Zoning and Sign Permits

If you are going to set up your business in your home, you need to research local zoning laws. Since redesign is performed at a client's home, the traffic to and from your home office is kept to a minimum. Therefore, cities may allow such businesses to be home-based.

However, they may have restrictions regarding your business, such as signage laws. You also need to look into any neighborhood covenants that may be in place. Your neighborhood rules may be stricter than the government laws. You can find information regarding zoning and sign permits by inquiring at your local town or city planning board.

Opening Your Business Bank Account

When considering a bank, look at the following:

- **A bank that is close to your place of business.** This will make depositing and withdrawing funds easier.

- **The charges that apply for various services.** Services may incur fees if you drop below a set minimum balance, if you write more than a certain number of checks, or if you go beyond a certain number of teller visits. Consider all these fees carefully — it really can add up.

- **Size.** Smaller, local banks take more time to help new businesses in their community. Larger, national banks have more services. Look at both kinds of banks to determine your needs and how they fit their offered services.

After you have selected a bank, set up your business account and order checks and extra deposit slips. Finally, make a point to get to know the bank personnel on a first-name basis and establish a relationship. You do not know when their assistance may come in handy.

Insurance

Because redesign, redecorating, and real estate staging is a relatively new business form, be sure to explain in depth to your insurance provider just what kind of service you provide for your client. Let him know that your job may include:

- Moving around items that belong to the client in the client's home

- Hanging pictures on walls

- Moving furniture

- Driving to the client's home with items that you have purchased for the client

- Standing on a ladder in the client's home

- Driving your car with your client as a passenger to shop in local stores

- Renting furniture that may be used in your client's home

Then, you will want to discuss the different types of insurance that may be considered.

Car Insurance: Whether your business owns one car or a fleet of vehicles, automobile insurance protects your business for damage caused to other people or property by your vehicle, as well as damage to your own. If the vehicles are damaged in an accident or stolen, the business has to repair or replace them. If there is an accident and the business is at fault, the business may be subject to large claims from people injured in the accident. A business auto insurance policy helps cover both property and liability risks that businesses face because of the ownership or use of autos and trucks.

As a home-based business owner, you may use the same auto for business and pleasure. You will need to decide whether to buy a commercial auto or personal auto insurance policy. In many cases, if you use your vehicle to deliver goods or services or to transport your equipment from job to job, you need only your current personal auto policy.

Property Insurance: Property insurance protects the contents of your business against fire, theft, and other perils. There are different types of property insurance and levels of coverage available. Property insurance can be tailored to fit your needs since no two businesses are the same.

Liability Insurance: Liability insurance covers the cost of lawsuits stemming from accidents that cause bodily injury or property damage and other miscellaneous claims, such as libel, slander, and false advertising. Liability will pay not only the cost of the damages but also the attorney fees and other costs associated with your defense in a lawsuit, whether or not the lawsuit has merit.

For example, what if you broke a valuable vase? Rather than pay for it yourself, your insurance policy would cover that loss. If you have elected to become a sole proprietor, you can be covered with an addendum on your home insurance policy.

The best place to start when seeking insurance is with your current insurance carrier. Properly insuring your redesign business will protect you and your family from financial loss.

Office Administration — The Musts of a Well-Run Business

Consistency

In the beginning, your business will be small enough that remembering all you have to do in a day is easy. You will have no problem remembering your clients or their phone numbers. Simple lists will keep things flowing easily. Eventually, however, you will need to incorporate business standards and practices.

There is no time like the beginning to set up these systems. You may not have the need for them in the beginning, but that is when you have the time for the development.

Avoid This Business Blunder

My business was so small that I felt I did not need to have a form just for recording a client's information. In fact, I felt that I did not need a form or a standard process for anything. Besides, as a creative type, a form was very restrictive. I did not want a form telling me what to write and where to write it.

Therefore, I used pretty paper of different sizes and shapes, sticky notes, or even scraps of paper from the back of a notebook. I enjoyed it. I felt free.

If I wanted to review something, I could even think to myself, "I wrote it on the pink sticky note in the upper left corner in blue ink." Sure enough, there

---

Avoid This Business Blunder

it was. I was proud of myself for a while for not be being "all business" — until the day came that I did not remember.

I had several clients and several projects going on at one time, and that little scrap of paper was nowhere to be found. For that matter, I could not even remember if it was a scrap of paper, the note on the edge of a map, or the pink sticky note.

I had to go through many of these situations before concluding that, if I would "restrict" myself by using a form or a process, I could "free" myself from the frustration and move on with the work I enjoyed.

Keeping Client Records

Without your clients, you have no business. Therefore, keeping up with your clients — who they are, where they live, what they want, and why they want it — is an essential element of your business. Keeping up with this information requires record keeping in the form of client contact forms and client folders.

The contact sheet helps you get information from the first phone call. It will include the client's name, address, phone numbers, e-mails, and possibly family member names.

1. How clients like to be contacted is important. E-mail is the best way as long as they check their e-mail daily. If they do not, you will need to use the phone.

2. A marketing question that you must know is "How did you hear about my business?" Knowing this helps you put your money into marketing efforts that are working.

3. One of the best questions to ask is "Why are you calling today?" It is important because the answer is what you will refer to as you explain what you can do for them.

4. Finally, you will want space to take notes.

A client contact sheet is placed on the front of the file. A copy may also be placed inside the file.

Example Client Contact Sheet
Name: _____
Spouse and/or children's names and ages: _____ _____ _____
Address:_____ _____
How did you hear of us? _____
Home phone number: _____
Office number: _____
Fax number: _____
Cell number: _____
E-mail: _____
Why are you calling today? _____
How do you like to be contacted? _____
Notes: _____ _____ _____

In addition to the contact sheet information (Appendix 12), you will want to gather further information for the client's folder on the Pre-Appointment Question form (Appendix 13) by asking the following questions:

- Can you tell me a bit about what you are looking for?

- Did you just move into town? If so, from where?

- Have you ever had redesign/redecorating/real estate staging work done before?

- What kind of concerns do you have?

- What are you thinking of investing?

- When do you anticipate having all the information necessary to make your decision?

- When would be a good time for both you and your spouse to meet with me?

These questions do not have to be asked in this order, nor do all of them have to be answered in the first phone conversation. It is important, however, to get to these questions eventually because the answers will help both you and your potential client determine if a working relationship will be of value.

Mary's Trade Tips

Having these forms is also useful when and if you are working with a partner or have hired an administrative assistant. In this way, you are sure to get the required information.

In addition to the contact form and pre-appointment question form, your client's file will contain the following information:

- Measurements

- Digital photos — labeled

- Measurable statistics

Measurable statistics, such as the number of phone calls before having a commitment to a redesign project or the length of time between a commitment and completion, are valuable numbers to have.

These are statistics to let you know what to be aware of next time so you can control your business. You want to know when a project got started, the date of the first estimate, the date of the actual project, and the date you were paid.

As you get started in this business, you may think you are going to talk to a client and you are going to have immediate work. The truth is, it might take up to six weeks before you begin work with a client. There is a lot of lag time.

Once you know the numbers, however, you can figure out what you can do to shorten the amount of project time. You also can determine what you want to do while a project is in the lag time.

For more example forms see Appendix 11, 16, and 17.

Keeping Financial Records

Your ultimate goal is to run a profitable business so you can stay in business and continue to offer your services to those who need them. You can only do this if you stay in touch with where your money is coming from and, more importantly, where your money is going.

Many of your business expenses can be written off as taxes. Good record keeping can save you money, and it definitely will be to your advantage if you were ever to be audited by the IRS.

Having record keeping systems in place before you open is

highly advised, even if it is a simple hand ledger book with two columns, listing the money that comes in and the money that goes out.

In the most straightforward way, you need to keep track of your business revenues — the money that comes in — and your business expenses — the money that goes out.

The most important thing to do concerning financial record keeping is to retain your receipts.

For a simple filing system, you can do the following:

- Use an expandable folder that can house 13 files. Label one folder "Revenue and Expense Report" and the other folders each month of the year.

- Start with the month that you are in — for example, January. Every day in January, collect your receipts for the day.

- Record your expenses, either in your weekly balance sheet you are filling out manually or in a spreadsheet you have developed. Eventually you will want to use a commercial accounting computer program, such as QuickBooks.

- Record any sales you make.

- File all your receipts for the month in order.

- Switch to a new file every month.

- File your weekly Revenue and Expense Report in its file. In the end, you will have 52 reports in chronological order.

Expense Sheet Week of May 21, 2007

Money I spent on the business:

• Do not forget to include rent, electricity, phone, advertising, and so forth. Keep all of your receipts.

Day	Where?	Item	Amount	What	Or for Whom?
Mon. May 21	Piper's Tavern	Lunch	12.50	Met with Susie, new client	
	Staples	Paper and ink	72.00	Office supplies	
	TJ Maxx	Accessories	148.00		For Thurs. redesign with Amy
Tues. May 22	No purchases				
Wed. May 23	No purchases				
Thurs. May 24	No purchases				
Fri. May 25	BP	Gas	46.00	Auto	
Sat. May 26	No purchases				
Sun. May 27	No purchases				
Total			278.50		

Income Sheet Week of May 21, 2007

Money that came into the business

Day	From	Amount	For What?
Mon. May 21			
Tues. May 22			
Wed. May 23			
Thurs. May 24	Amy	550.00	Redesign

Income Sheet Week of May 21, 2007			
	Amy	95.00	Items purchased for redesign
Fri. May 25			
Sat. May 26			
Sun. May 27			
Total		645.00	

Check Appendix 18 for a Revenue and Expense Report template.

Home Office Deductions

If you use a portion of your home for business purposes on a "regular and exclusive" basis, you may be able to take a home-office deduction.

By the IRS definition, exclusive means you have dedicated a specific area of your home to conducting your business or trading or meeting with clients or customers. When the agency says regular, it means the area is used regularly for your business. Incidental or occasional business use is not regular use. You do not meet the requirements of exclusive business use if the area in question is used for both business and personal purposes.

Expenses you may be able to deduct for business use of the home include:

- Utilities
- Depreciation
- Insurance
- Painting and repairs
- A portion of your home's real estate taxes
- Mortgage interest or rent

To find out what qualifies as a deductible business expense go to **http://www.irs.gov/smallbiz** and search for "business expenses."

••⌘••

Mary's Trade Tips

Be careful not to confuse personal expenses with business expenses when claiming home-office deductions. The IRS says taxpayers commonly claim their basic local telephone service as a deduction. The first telephone line into a home is a nondeductible personal expense. However, charges for long-distance business phone calls on that line are deductible. You also can deduct the cost of a second line into a home used exclusively for business.

Your deductions in these expense categories are determined by the percentage of your home used to conduct your small business. Computing the business percentage is easy.

Divide the area used for your business by the total area of the home. You also can divide the number of rooms used for business by the total number of rooms in the home if all rooms are similar sizes.

For example, if you have a 2,000-square-foot home and use 250 square feet for your business, the business percentage would be:

250 / 2,000 = 0.125 x 100 = 12.5 percent

To determine your home-office deduction, multiply the percentage of your home used for business by your allowable indirect household expenses, like electricity and gas. Then you add your direct expenses. In the example above, 12.5 percent of your indirect expenses are deductible.

To fully understand the IRS rules in this area, you need to read Publication 587 "Business Use of Your Home." The publication is available at **http://www.irs.gov** or by calling 800-829-3676.

If you claim a home-office deduction, you should keep meticulous records of all your expenses and be prepared to back them up if you are asked to by the IRS. As with most tax matters, it is a good idea to check with a certified public accountant or tax attorney if you have any questions.

Your Small Shopping List of Essentials

The beauty of a redesign, redecorating, and real estate staging business is that you just need the basics to get the business off the ground. Completing a project for satisfied clients takes little more than your natural talent.

There is a need to have traditional office supplies, but much of what you will need to get started is already in your home. Resist the urge to shop for the office. Instead, plan to spend money on things, such as marketing, that will grow your business. The objective of your business is to make money, not spend it.

Nonetheless, there are items you will need to start your business.

Dedicated Phone Line

Every home has a telephone. Therefore, it is easy to ignore the need for a dedicated business line as a way of saving money. Do not fall into this trap. Nothing says "unprofessional" like having your seven-year-old answer your phone or having your voicemail pick up with a message that says, "Thanks for calling the Larsen family."

Having a dedicated phone line does not mean that you have to install a physical phone and phone line into your home. You can establish a business phone number and have it permanently forwarded to your business cell phone. Doing so allows you to have a phone number listed in the yellow pages as a business.

Make sure your cell phone receives service in your home office before using this option.

Voicemail

As your business grows, you will find yourself out of the home office more than you are in it. Therefore, it is important to have an answering machine or voicemail service to pick up missed calls.

Make sure your voicemail reflects the fact that you are a business. Do not just say, "This is Mary, and I am not here right now." You want to make sure that, when people call, they know they have called the right place.

Be sure to leave a professional message that lets the client know when to expect a return call from you. Also be sure to request the needed information from the prospective client. If you have a byline as part of your business, such as "Every Home Has a Story to Tell," be sure to use it in your message as well. You may even want to direct the caller to your Web site for further information.

Sample Voicemail Message

"Thank you for calling Mary Larsen Designs where every home has a story to tell. I am so sorry to have missed your call, but I am out making someone's home beautiful. Please leave your name and number so I can get back to you. I will be returning calls between the hours of ten a.m. and noon. You also can visit **www.MaryLasenDesigns.com** for more information. I look forward to speaking with you!"

Computer and Printer

A computer is essential to your business for e-mail, client, and financial files and desktop publishing.

Your clients may want to correspond with you by e-mail. Therefore, you will need a computer to both send and receive e-mail on a regular basis. Having an e-mail address that reflects your business is a good idea. For instance, you might use **redesignbymary@aol.com**. Once you have a Web site, you can have an e-mail through your hosting company. For instance, you might use **mary@marylarsendesigns.com**.

Any financial bookkeeping also can be done on your computer. You can use a software program, such as a QuickBooks, or develop your own spreadsheet for tracking your money. Software programs for client contacts are also available. See Appendix 20 for software and computer class ideas.

Desktop publishing will help you keep your initial operating costs low. For instance, printing your own stationery will keep you from having to purchase it retail. Most computers come with a graphics program you can use for any printing needs.

Fax Machine

A fax machine in your home office can be quite handy. You may want to consider getting a computer printer that is multifunctional and works as a printer, copier, fax machine, and scanner. It will save on desktop space and give you the luxury of having a fax machine for printed documents if your e-mail is down or if you are dealing with a business that is fax-driven. Accessory and furniture manufacturing companies still may be fax-driven, which would affect your business if your business grows to include these products.

Another option is to go to **www.efax.com**. eFax is an online fax service that eliminates the need for a fax machine, an extra fax line, and all the associated expenses, such as paper and ink. You will get a real fax number tied to your e-mail. To the person faxing you, it looks and acts like any other fax number. When someone faxes to your number, the fax is converted to a file that is e-mailed to you as an attachment.

Files and Filing Cabinet

Even the simplest jobs will generate a file folder. Once that folder is created, you have to be able to file it somewhere. If you do not have room for a filing cabinet, there are great filing systems at your local office supply store, such as Staples, Office Max, or Office Depot.

Digital Camera

You will find that potential clients love good before and after pictures of your work and that these pictures, therefore, are crucial to the development and growth of your business. To take these photographs, you will need a good digital camera.

If you have not purchased a digital camera yet, consider buying one with a 28mm lens or one that will accept a wide-angle converter lens. A camera with a 24mm lens is the minimum for photographing interiors. Most point-and-shoot cameras, the kind you slip into your purse, will not take good interior photographs because the field of view is too narrow. In other words, you can photograph only a small portion of the room, and you will lose the effect of the entire redesign project.

Some cameras do not have a wide enough lens but do take wide lens converters. Converters adapt to the camera lens to extend its wide-angle range to at least 24mm.

You also will want to purchase a camera with a hot shoe. This is a plug-in for an external flash. The flash built into digital cameras is not strong enough for interior photographs. Therefore, having a larger one that you can attach to the camera is essential.

The preferred cameras for interior photos are the Canon Powershots (G series, Pro 1) or the Nikon Coolpix line. You can inquire at a camera store about these cameras or shop for them online.

••◆⌘◆••
_____

Mary's Trade Tips

Digital cameras make taking interior photos amazingly easy but only if you have taken the time to read the camera's manual. Take one Saturday afternoon to read the manual and practice the different steps and functions. Once you know how to use your camera, taking great before and after shots of your redesign jobs will be a breeze.

_____

Office Supply List

Instead of heading to your local office supply store, look around the house to find the supplies you need for the office. Remember, you do not have a storefront, so no one will see that the stapler is ten years old or that you are using an old hotel pen for taking notes.

Here is a list of basics so that can get you started:

- Pens and pencils
- Notepads
- File folders
- White out
- Stapler and staples
- Paperclips
- Calculator
- Printer paper

- Business envelopes
- Tape
- Ruler
- Stamps
- Scissors

Tools of the Trade

Although you need few items to complete your first redesign project, there are tools of the trade that are helpful. As your business grows, you will create a central toolkit that goes with you wherever you go, as well as "specialty" toolkits for your add-ons, such as a toolkit for window treatments or a toolkit for painting (Appendix 4).

These are the tools you will find especially helpful:

- Screwdriver
- Scissors
- Wire cutter
- Step stool
- Sharpie marker
- Straight and safety pins
- Rubber bands
- Painter's tape
- Floral sheers and tape
- Flashlight
- Masking and Scotch tape
- Pencil and chalk
- Mark-it level
- Museum or poster putty
- Hammer, nails, picture-hanging wire, wall anchors, and picture-hanging kit
- Rechargeable cordless drill and batteries
- Furniture movers for both carpet and hardwoods
- Furniture touch-up sticks or pens
- Lint brush and wrinkle-release spray

- Other items for decorating: greenery, floral foam, plate stands, old books, fabric scraps, small accessories, curtain rods and rings, sheer drapes

Your Car — Your Mobile Office

You might be surprised at how quickly your car becomes your mobile office. Since all your projects will begin and end on site, you car will have to carry everything you need.

You will be bringing items to your client's home depending on the particular project. Everything you bring has to get from your house to his house. The best way to do that is to always have it together in one toolbox or toolkit. Additionally, all these items need to be organized so that you know where to find your tools or other project items.

Eventually, a minivan, an SUV, or a car with a large trunk will be the most useful.

Team Members

Even if you are a single-owner business, as a redesigner, redecorator, and real estate stager, you may find that you need help from time to time — you need a team. Rather than hiring employees for your business, consider working with individuals who are in business for themselves as a subcontractor. You do not want to deal with 1099s, employee taxes, and insurance. It also will be advantageous to you if these team members do their own billing and invoicing.

Members of your team might include:

- Drapery installers
- Heavy picture installers

- Furniture movers
- Handyman
- Plumber
- General contractors
- Painters – interior and exterior

••✦⌘✦••

Mary's Trade Tips

Have a good list of team members whom you work with consistently and who are professional and reliable. A value you bring to the client is having the experience of working with these dependable people. The client will not have to rely on finding contractors through the yellow pages.

Just Start — You Can Never Be Ready

It is easy to get caught up in the tasks of running your business since you are going to be not only a redesigner but a sales manager, marketing manager, bookkeeper, administrative assistant, Web designer, and public speaker as well. Therefore, you put together your to-do lists and never seem to get them all done.

There is a reason that large companies have departments to handle the various aspects of a business. Each facet is a full-time job on its own. In the beginning stages of your business, you will not have the luxury of hiring out these tasks and must take them on yourself.

Be aware that it is easy to use the "business" aspect of your work as a procrastination tool. The individual pieces have to be done, but the question is when.

Is it necessary to have a three-page, full-color brochure ready before you tell all your friends and neighbors that you are in business? Do you have to have a full-blown computer accounting software program before you can accept a check for your services?

The answers are no. You will never be completely ready to start. There always will be one more task that could be completed. Do not let this stop you. Get the basics done, jump in, and begin your business.

Avoid This Business Blunder

I recently worked with a woman who was just launching her redesign business. When I asked her why she thought she needed a business coach, she said she was not ready to begin her business but wanted to be ready — with clients — at the end of 90 days.

As a business coach, one of the first things I do with a new client is assess his or her business as it stands today, in order to establish the areas in which we need to focus.

As we went over the assessment, I became increasingly puzzled as to why she wanted to work with me. Virtually every item listed under my "launching your business" category had been completed successfully. In fact, she had several items completed that I have listed under my "been in business a couple of years" category.

So again, I asked her why she wanted to work with me, and again she responded with, "Because I am not ready."

After a little conversation, it was obvious she was not going to be ready any time soon. It was not because the business aspects of her work were not covered; it was because she was hiding behind her tasks — the things she "had to do before she possibly could start her business."

I tried to impress upon my coaching client that she could launch her business today. She could e-mail all her contacts and let them know she was open for business. She could call her five closest friends and ask them to call their five

Avoid This Business Blunder

closest friends. She could pass out her beautiful flyers in her neighborhood this afternoon. We also talked about how you never can be, nor should you ever really be, ready. There is always something new to try and something new to do. Have faith in what you have done to date and get started now.

It turns out she was right after all. She was not ready, and she has yet to launch her business.

Getting ready for business takes planning but is well worth the effort. Another piece of your plan that is worth the effort is marketing. The next chapter will give you marketing tools aimed specifically toward the redesign, redecorating, and real estate staging business.

Chapter 5

Marketing, Media, and More

$\mathcal{U}$ pon the launching of your business you will see quickly that you are running two businesses — the business of the service you provide and the business of the marketing of that service. Marketing is the key to making your business grow.

Marketing identifies, addresses, and answers your customer's needs. Be prepared to put yourself in the customer's shoes and make sure that satisfying his needs is what your business is doing.

Not understanding what your clients want is the reason so many small businesses fail. People are willing to pay you if you can satisfy their needs and desires and remove their frustrations, fears, or concerns.

It is important that you do not assume that marketing a business is quick and easy. It takes work, patience, and constant, consistent, and dedicated effort.

The following marketing tools are excellent ways to grow your business from a $500-a-month hobby to a six-figure business.

Who Knows You, Not Who You Know

Everything is a marketing opportunity. This is especially true as you start your business. Your business is about you and what you do; therefore, everyone you meet and everywhere you go is an opportunity to market your business.

When you are in business for yourself, you are the only person who can make this happen. People already know and like you, and they may already trust you. You might be doing them a disservice by not letting them know about the services you offer. They might be struggling at this exact moment to find someone who does exactly what you do, and they would be relieved to know that, at the very least, they can talk to you about their needs.

Consider everything you do as a marketing opportunity. When you go to a meeting, make it a point that at least two new people know what you do before you leave. Make it a point to meet the person in front of you at the grocery store or the grocery store clerk. The clerk meets people during the day, and one of them is bound to mention they are looking for someone who does just what you do.

Every time you interact with the public, make it a point that one more person will know what you do. In the end, it is not who you know but who knows you.

Do They Really Know What You Do?

Starting your new business is exciting. You have researched, studied, and immersed yourself in every aspect of redesign, redecorating, and home staging. This consumes you. Therefore, it is understandable that you believe everyone around you knows what you do and why you are doing it. The truth is that they do not and will not unless you tell them.

Avoid This Business Blunder

I have a mastermind group of friends that I meet with every six weeks. These five women are the smartest, funniest group of women I know. They are amazing people. In my mind, I thought they knew everything about me.

They knew when I started my new business, and, of course, congratulations were made all around. As we met every six weeks, we all gave our business updates.

A year and a half into my business, one of them asked me, "Do you do custom bedding and pillows?"

I almost fell out of my chair. Custom work with fabric is a large part of my business. If my mastermind group did not know the answer to that question, then who did?

Nobody knows what you do. It is your job to say what you do in such a way that the person can respond to you.

The words "I am an interior decorator" bring up different connotations and create confusion. Saying, "I help people get their homes together. I can do anything to help them" also creates confusion. You will not do everything. Clients will hear what you say in relation to their problems. If their issue is that their sink is clogged and you have said you can do anything to help them with their home, they will want you to be the plumber.

Instead, you might say:

I work with busy, overextended homeowners who are frustrated that their home just does not feel finished.

Or

I specialize in turning a homeowner's overwhelming, unmanageable home decorating projects into a personal, satisfying experience – turning their home into their favorite place on Earth.

In addition to getting out there and telling people who you are and what you do, there are other marketing tools to help you grow your business. Here are some that are easy and inexpensive. Remember, you do not have to do every one before starting your business (see two letter samples in Appendix 9 and 10).

Using Your Client Base

Testimonials

As soon as you are through with a job, you need to make getting a testimonial letter from your satisfied client a high priority. In fact, before you start a job, tell your new client that your intention is to do such a great job that he happily will write a testimonial letter once the job is done. The problem can be twofold:

1. Once clients are through with your services, they are really through with you. You are no longer on their

mind. This is not because they did not appreciate your services but because their life is going on.

2. They write a letter, but it does not really convey what you want it to convey. It is too general. "XYZ did a great job. We really appreciate her work. Thank you." A good testimonial letter will use words that are more descriptive and state the benefits of working with you. Otherwise, they all end up sounding the same. You want a testimonial to talk about the results, such as "XYZ Designers gave me the home I have always wanted." You want them to talk about the bottom line.

Testimonial Examples

Here are three different testimonials that go beyond the "thank you" and "you did a nice job" varieties.

Mary! Everyone LOVED, LOVED, LOVED the kitchen. One of my dearest friends, who is over nearly every other day, has something new to say about it everyday … the lighting is so much better in here now, I love the way the window treatments draw your eye to this level of the room, or I am so glad we no longer have to look at that *%$*^% house next door when we're in here.

And my husband Erik thought it looked very nice. He is not one to jump up and down like I tend to do, but he was definitely pleased with the look and the way the room turned out!

And of course, people were asking for your info!

Thank you, thank you, thank you.

Count me among your fans and 150 percent satisfied customers. What can we do next?!?!?

C.P. from Cary, North Carolina

Testimonial Examples

Mary — A huge thank you for all of your ideas, guidance, and especially patience in our kitchen remodel! It makes me happy every time I walk in my door.

Please stop by soon to see it again in all its glory. The kids would love to see you, too!

A.A. from Apex, North Carolina

Dear Mary,

Our new bonus room is incredible! The colors and textures are gorgeous, and I do not know who loves it more — my kids or my husband. And speaking of my kids, Jack loves his bedroom so much he has been asking to go to bed early! Who knew that a beautifully decorated room would get my child to bed on time with no fight!

Thank you so much for that, too!

M.R. from Raleigh, North Carolina

There are two ways to get the kind of testimonial you need. One way is to get a public relations/marketing person to talk with your client and then draft a testimonial letter based on her comments. The other way is to listen carefully to what your client has to say and write up a testimonial based on her comments. Either way, share it with your client and ask if she would be willing to sign the letter and, with her permission, use it on your advertising materials. Clients are more than happy to help.

If you wait for your client to give you a testimonial without prompting, you will be left with little to show prospective clients. It is only natural that you are no longer on her mind. Getting the testimonial while she still is thinking about how you helped her is not only the best time to get a testimonial but perhaps the only time.

Word of Mouth

There are reasons why word-of-mouth marketing is extremely successful. Those passing your information along are not giving a sales pitch. Instead, they are giving a recommendation based on their personal experience. You cannot buy their authenticity, their passion, their commitment, and their willingness to volunteer their time passing along your information to those they know.

A word-of-mouth referral comes with a high degree of trust compared to other advertising methods. The more trust your prospect has in you, the easier it is to sell him or her your service. People do business with people they have confidence in.

••⌘••
Mary's Trade Tips

It does not work to say, "Tell your friends about me." Your clients are just like you. They are busy and work all day. They may think the room is beautiful, but they may not take the time to call a friend and say so unless the conversation happens to turn to redesign.

Instead, ask them to give you a name. For example, "Can you think of someone, just like you, that would love to have her room look beautiful but just does not have the time to do it herself?" When they say yes and give you a name, ask them to tell that person about you. "Can you tell Lisa about your room and then give her my information?" Now, instead of waiting for a conversation with Lisa to turn to redesign, your client is more likely to call Lisa and tell her about you.

Referral Programs

Offering a free gift, a gift certificate, or a discount on future services to current clients will create an incentive for them to bring you referrals. Offering cash for referrals might not be a good idea — people want to feel their testimonials are given freely and not coerced or paid for. Send your customers or clients a letter or e-mail asking for their help. Good clients will have no problem referring you to others.

Your Name in Print

Business Cards

Business cards are the cheapest and most under-used marketing tool in business. If you are not making them work for you, you may be missing an excellent opportunity.

You should have your cards with you wherever you go. There is no reason to ever leave home without them. Every opportunity is a marketing opportunity. When you talk with someone about your business, you can pull out your card.

When you first get started in your business, do not buy your cards in large quantities. You may change your name, your logo, or the services you offer. Your obsolete cards still will be valid because your information will be the same, but it is not worth getting a discount to get so many cards when you most likely will change them. You might consider printing your own business cards in small quantities on your home computer.

Avoid This Business Blunder

I started my business and came up with a great name and logo. I called myself Larsen – Trochlil Designs, using both my married and maiden name. I spent about 50 cents a card (which included the design of the logo), and the card was beautiful! Everyone said so! The logo caught your attention, and everyone wanted to talk about the interesting name.

Avoid This Business Blunder

The problem was that no one could pronounce, remember, or spell my interesting name. It was bad enough if someone wanted to find me in the phonebook, and even worse when it came to my Web site. Therefore, I changed my business name to Mary Larsen Designs and created a different logo. Luckily, all the contact information is staying the same for my business, so I still will be able to use the old cards until the new cards are ready. I really should have purchased a much smaller quantity to begin with.

919.773.1445   3340 Langston Circle, Apex, NC 27539
www.MaryLarsenDesigns.com   Mary@MaryLarsenDesigns.com

Every business card should have the following:

- **The name of your company and your logo**. When you first get started, you may not have a logo. Do not worry about it. When you do get one, you can print new cards.

- **Your contact information.** This includes your telephone number, your cell number if it is different from your business number, your fax, your e-mail, and your mailing address.

- **Your Internet URL.** Having a Web site is necessary when you begin your business. Your URL, such as **www .marylarsendesigns.com**, should be on everything you print.

- **Your byline.** Add a short statement about what you do, such as "Transforming Your Home in Just One Day."

You can also add a branding type tagline such as "Every Home Has a Story to Tell."

- **Add color.** People like color. As a redesigner, your clients will expect you to be creative. Going beyond black and white will help your card stand out.

••⌘••
_____

Mary's Trade Tips

Try to develop a catchy phrase that relates to who you are. Mary Larsen Designs really is not catchy. But my tagline — "Every home has a story to tell" — is great! It immediately brings a picture to your mind, and the saying rolls right off your tongue.

Jane Pollack is an extremely talented woman who creates Ukrainian painted eggs. People call her the egg lady. Early in her career, it drove her crazy because she is a great artist. She does fabulous work. Finally, she got over what they called her and was happy that everyone knew who she was — it brought in business!

Do not worry about being caught in a title. In the design world, I know the blind lady, the zipper lady, and the pillow lady. Who cares what you are known by, as long as you are known.

_____

Now that you have your business cards, here are business card marketing tips and tricks:

- **Always hand out two business cards** — one for the prospect and one for him to hand out to a colleague.

- **Leave your business cards everywhere you go** — leave one on the table in a restaurant or post them on community bulletin boards.

- **Include business cards with your invoices or bill payments.**

- **Tuck one of your business cards inside library books related to your services.**

- **Use your business card as a ballot for contests and drawings at events.**

Business cards are wonderful advertising tools because you can target when and where you leave them or to which individuals you hand them in order to get the greatest advantage. Of course, there is not a guarantee that leaving them will result in sales. The idea is to increase awareness of your business so that the recipient will think of you when he needs your service.

Postcards

There are times when you would like to leave a potential client with something, but a business card is too small and a tri-fold brochure is too expensive. One good solution is a postcard.

Your postcard should be full-color and have either two to three "after" photos or one set of "before and after" photos. Be sure to include your logo and contact information on the front.

The back side also will have your contact information and a call to action, such as "Call Today for a Design Consultation."

Although you will use these postcards mainly as a giveaway at short presentations or for clients to give to their friends, they also can be used as a direct mail marketing tool.

Stationary

If you go to your local office supply store and tell the employees that you are going to open a business, they will hand you a brochure containing all the different printed materials you will need to get started. Stationery will be on that list. In the redesign business (in fact, in any small business), you do not need all the stationery people say you need.

As with business cards, you can create your stationery using inexpensive desktop publishing software. Since you are a designer, your printed material should have color. Keep in mind, however, that going beyond three colors becomes too overwhelming for the eye.

You also need to consider paper quality. People expect nice-quality paper when you are sending them a thank-you note or a letter that confirms an appointment (Appendix 4). On the other hand, they do not expect nice-quality paper when they get a bill.

Flyers

Leaving flyers in a neighborhood can be a good idea but only if you have other marketing going on that will reach the same people. Potential clients need to see your name seven times or more before they are going to know who you are and consider working with you.

Flyers are more effective if you can put a client's name on them and then only if you use them in the neighborhood where that client lives. Of course, you must be sure to get your client's permission before passing these out.

This kind of flyer might say:

Hi! I'm Mary Larsen of Mary Larsen Designs. I just redesigned Suzy Smith's living room. If you want to see what I've done for Suzy and what I can do for you, give her a call at 555-1234.

These kinds of flyers will get you business. Other flyers with no personal endorsement will end up in the trash.

••⌘••
Mary's Trade Tips

Putting out flyers once a week for seven weeks can make you money, but the time and expense can be large. A better idea might be to send a postcard home with the friends of your children and ask them to give it to their mom. You are more likely to get into their home because they know you.

Sign in the Yard

You are driving down the road and see a sign in the yard. It is a sign that says Roofing by XYZ Company, Landscaping by XYZ Company, or Siding by XYZ Company. You can do the same thing. Have a sign that says, "Home Redesigned by Mary Larsen Designs."

Signs are inexpensive. You can have a beautiful sign made for $50. They capture attention, and they get your name known in the community.

Do not forget to put your name, phone number, and Web address (in big letters so that it can be seen from the road) on your sign.

Your Computer Presence

E-mail

Having an e-mail address is essential in today's world. You will find that a large number of your clients will wish to be contacted by e-mail rather than by phone. There are two things you need to do to make your e-mail effective:

1. Have an e-mail name that fits your company. (See the section "Computer and Printer" in Chapter 4.)

2. Have a business signature on your e-mail that has your name, phone number, and URL.

E-mail Signature Example

-Mary Larsen
Mary Larsen Designs, Inc.
Because every home has a story to tell™
www.MaryLarsenDesigns.com
Designing Your Success™
www.GrowYourDesignBiz.com
3340 Langston Circle
Apex, NC 27539
919-773-1445
Mary@MaryLarsenDesigns.com

Web site

Although many marketing tactics can wait, a Web site is a tool that you need to use immediately. A Web site can have multiple pages, like those at **www.marylarsendesigns.com**, or it can be a single page that looks more like a giant business card with your business name, your logo, your contact information, and a quick synopsis of the services you provide.

People search the Internet when they need a designer. They might search using words like "interior design" or "redesign" or "redecorate" or "home staging." If they are redecorating, they may even use words like "color" or "window treatments." These words are called keywords.

The best way to create a Web site is to hire a Web designer. A single-page Web site will not be costly, and Web designers know how to use the right keywords so that those searching for your services can find you.

Since you will not have a storefront, your Web site presence is crucial. It will be your storefront to the world.

Avoid This Business Blunder

Having a Web presence is essential. However, it is very important that you portray the right kind of presence. MySpace and other group entries are searchable through all the major search engines. Do not place your non-business life online, especially if it does not look good in relation to your profession.

Be sure that your Web site shows that you are creative. An uncreative, carelessly put together Web site may make people believe you do not have the ability to redesign their homes.

Another thing to be careful about is color. Color means different things to different people, and certain colors are almost universally viewed as harsh or irritating, such as electric orange. Appendix 22 has a list of the traditional meanings of color.

Finally, be sure to display your business URL everywhere. Think of your Web site as a second office location. Any visitor should be able to get as much information from your Web site as he would if he walked in your front door. Your Web site gives your business credibility, so use it to your advantage.

If you do not have the money to hire a Web designer, you may want to consider creating a blog with only one entry. This entry will look like a one-page Web site. (To learn how to create a blog, read "Create a Blog" in Chapter 10.)

Getting Out in Public

Presentations

Presentations are just classes, seminars, or other ways to get in front of people in many different settings. Presentations help get you in front of people you do not know. The exciting thing is that they all know you when you are done.

After a presentation, one of those people you did not even meet will tell someone about you and what you do. You will not know him, but that is not important. What is important is he knows you.

••✦⌘✦••

Mary's Trade Tips

Start a program called "Girl's Night Out — Wine and Design." Provide free monthly classes to women that are fun and informative on the topic of decorating. Women of all ages come to learn about the month's lesson. Perhaps it is on color, window coverings, or furniture placement. If you make it fun, they will come. Once they come, they will learn about you and who you are. They are likely to use you when they need a stager or redesigner and may pass your name on to others who may need your service. How can you make it fun to be out for a night? Offer food, drinks, prizes, and useful information.

Teaching about what you do may seem counterintuitive. Why would you tell people what you know so they can go do it themselves without your help?

The answer is this:

1. By teaching, you are positioning yourself as an expert.

2. Those who take what you taught them and do it on their own were not going to be your clients anyway.

3. You have just shown a group what you can do. Those who watched your presentation may realize that you can make it look easy, but it will not be easy for them. They become your customers.

4. Those people in your class may not take you up on your offer of service but will be impressed with your professionalism and pass your name along.

One type of presentation to consider is a home party. It is a fabulous marketing tool. Ask a friend or client that you already have done work for to hold a party. It is more like an open house where her friends will get to see what you have done.

You will give a little talk. You will have free giveaways. When you are done, you will have ten people who heard about you, and you will have their contact information.

Avoid This Business Blunder

If you are a home-based design service business, it is very hard to place an ad that is effective. The ad is translated as a "store that has design services." Even when you phrase your ad in such a way that reads, "We come to you," the impression is that you are a store that people can come to.

Ads are very difficult to write to get a good response — being in front of people through presentations is much more effective for a design business.

Presentations are such an excellent marketing tool that an entire chapter, Chapter 6, is dedicated to the subject.

Networking Meetings

Networking is the art of making and using contacts. The goal of networking is not to instantly get new customers and clients. The purpose of networking is to create a pool of people who can help you grow your business through the people they know and the services they offer.

Networking is a two-way street. When you meet someone, ask him about his business and take a genuine interest. When you take a sincere interest in someone else, he will take interest in you. When the time seems appropriate, tell him about your business. Create a short, snappy statement that is intriguing and makes people want to learn more about you.

Networking Example

Short Introduction

I work with busy, overextended homeowners who are frustrated that their home just does not feel finished. I specialize in turning their overwhelming, unmanageable home decorating projects into a personal, satisfying experience — turning their home into their favorite place on Earth.

30-Second Introduction, Also Known as an "Elevator Speech"

My name is Mary Larsen, and I am the owner of Mary Larsen Designs, a full-service interior design firm. We do everything from furniture to accessories, area rugs, and even new home construction and specialize in custom window treatments. We cater to business professionals who want the success of their career to be reflected in the interior of their home or business.

Networking Example

We work on the principle that every home has a story to tell — a unique story — and we guarantee that, just like a good book, you will enjoy the design process from start to finish and especially love the ending.

We would love to work with you and your friends and help you discover the things important to you to tell your home's story.

Who is the next person you know who needs help with her home?

I would like you to think about the next person you know who could benefit from my services: someone who is just moving into a home and may need blinds or someone who has lived in her home and needs help pulling it all together. After the meeting, I would love to talk with you about her.

A network is not a collection of business cards but of people. One of the best things you can do with the people you network with is to be a connector. Connect them with people you believe can help them out and help them further their goals. Remember that the purpose of networking is not to get your contact's business; instead, you are trying to get business from everyone this person knows.

Networking meetings need to be local since your business relies on local clientele. Consider the following events:

- Women's clubs
- Builder's associations
- Ruritans
- Chambers of Commerce
- The American Business Association
- Local city or town business associations
- Jaycees
- PTA
- Rotary clubs
- Garden clubs

You must get out and network. This is how people get to know you. To do this, you need to find out what networking events are in your area and attend them.

•♦❖♦•

Mary's Trade Tips

At your next networking event, ask if you can set up a small table with a display of ideas, including "before and after" photos. Seeing is believing.

———

Vendor's Show

Vendor show success is limited. It is hard to get a good client this way, and it is quite expensive. Redesign and redecorating is a personal and intimate service. It is not like getting someone to paint your house. People rarely pick someone for a personal service at a home show.

The best way to get something out of a vendor show is to go for the day and introduce yourself to all the other vendors. This way, you only have to pay for one ticket and not a vendor booth.

If you decide to try a home show, there are certain things you can do that will help you be more successful:

1. Why would anyone want to stop at your booth? What do you have to offer? One thing you can do is have a free giveaway.

2. Have your friends come by your booth to talk to you about your services. No one is going to stop first. This is group behavior. If you have people already at your booth, you can use group behavior to your advantage.

3. Do not have your giveaway bowl empty. Put in different business cards, so others will be prompted to add their card.

4. Vendor shows have e-mail lists. It might be worth paying a nominal fee to have access to this list.

5. Being a vendor will get your name listed on the show's advertising. This is often bigger advertising than you can do on your own.

One other way to make a vendor show profitable is to hold a class. You could talk about the benefits of home staging, picking the right paint colors, or the process of decluttering. Since home shows love something that will bring in customers, you may be able to teach the class without paying any money for a booth.

•♦⌘♦•

Mary's Trade Tips

At different times of the year, cities offer home tours. These tours may be for historic homes, builder award homes, or garden show homes. Consider asking to stage or redesign one of the rooms and then be there, in "your" room, during the tour. Those who see your lovely room can associate it with a real person and get a business card or handout of some kind. Though not entirely free, since you will have to do the work on the room, it can be worth your time.

Silent Auctions

Charities, groups, or schools raise money with a silent auction. Bidders offer money for the different items or services, and the highest bidder wins. You can participate in a silent auction by calling every school, church, or community organization. Those that have silent auctions will be happy to have you provide a one-hour consultation valued at your typical fee.

These organizations advertise their auctions and have your name printed in the program. More often than not, the person who wins your prize also will turn into a paying client.

•◆⌘◆•
Mary's Trade Tips

When contributing to a silent auction, call yourself by the name of your Web site. This means that the program will have you listed as **www.marylarsendesigns.com** *instead of Mary Larsen Designs. This gives those who take the program home with them an opportunity to look you up on the Internet.*

Volunteering

Find ways to volunteer in the community using your services. For instance, help decorate for a project like a Ronald McDonald house. Donate furnishings or accessories to a Habitat for Humanity house. These events get you in front of your community and show that you care about those who live near you.

Be sure to put these volunteering projects on your Web site and notify the public through news releases.

Becoming an Expert

Writing Articles

Article writing is great marketing tool that can establish you as an expert in your field. An article written by you is more meaningful and holds more credence than placing an advertisement.

If you are not an accomplished author, the idea of writing an article may sound daunting. You immediately ask, "What should I write about, how do I write about it, and who is going to read it?" Let us start with the first question.

Deciding what to write about is as easy as thinking about your last job. What questions did your client ask you? Whatever she asked is something she was thinking about right then. It is a timely topic. She may have said, "Wow! What made you think to put the sofa there?" The article might be, "Three Places You Never Considered Putting Your Sofa."

There is a reason you put the sofa there; now all you have to do is explain it. If you do not want to write it down, talk into a tape recorder. Explain what you did and why. Then take what you said and turn it into an article. This is a good way to help get the ideas flowing without having your hands frozen over the keyboard. You know the answer because you do this all day long.

•◆⌘◆•

Mary's Trade Tips

A great question to answer is this: "I have not worked with a redesigner before. What should I expect?"

Now it is time to get your article in print. Check with your local papers and free magazines. They look for content. There are also online sources that are constantly seeking new material. (See Appendix 19 for a list of online article submission sites.)

No matter where you have your article published, be sure to have an author biography listed at the end. This biography should contain a bit about who you are, what you do, and your contact information.

Newspaper Article Example

Pick a Color, Any Color

Mary Larsen, Correspondent

What is your greatest fear? Though this is surely something you should

Newspaper Article Example

think about on many levels, for home design the answer is almost always the same — color.

There is a good answer to why color is so scary for some of us: We react emotionally to color.

In fact, when I am doing home design for a home that will soon be for sale, one of the first elements that I must consider is the color of the interior walls. It needs to be a color that can appeal to the masses without evoking much of an emotion.

But the bottom line is that homes today are a refuge, your own personal refuge, and what you need to consider is how you want to feel. I ask clients if they have an idea of what colors they might want to use in a room. You may be surprised to know that seldom does a client state an actual color but instead almost invariably gives an emotion. "I want this room to be warm and soothing," or "I really want this room to be dynamic!" Color can affect that feeling greatly.

Along with the emotional impact, adding color to your home — especially your walls — can feel risky. It is common for people to think that white or off-white walls work with everything. So if your walls are off-white, all your furniture surely will go with it, right? That is not always true. As a backdrop for a room, white walls can create a stark, cold contrast to furniture and accessories, and when you consider the subtle undertones that white and off-white have, your room may not feel as if it "goes together," and you may not even realize why.

The reason to seriously consider color for your interior walls is this great emotional response that we have to color. How do you want to feel? And how do you want to feel in every room in your house?

To get started, here are common emotional responses to colors and room suggestions for use.

Room by Room

RED. It stimulates the senses. That is a reason we use red for Valentine's Day. It can suggest power, excitement, and attraction and is an appetite

Newspaper Article Example

stimulant. No wonder you always want dessert at your favorite red-decorated restaurant. Try it in your dining room.

ORANGE. It can suggest warmth and wholesomeness. Yet if the color is too intense, it can cause irritation and nervousness. Great for laundry rooms and craft rooms.

YELLOW. A pale shade of yellow suggests warmth and cheerfulness, but too much can fatigue your eyes. And beware of dingy yellow because it can make you feel somewhat under the weather. The right shades are beautiful throughout your home.

GREEN. Remember "green is serene." It is relaxing without being draining — soothing and refreshing at the same time. Perfect for an office or work space.

BLUE. America's overall favorite color, blue suggests peace, trust, and loyalty. It curbs your appetite and can lower your blood pressure. Great for living rooms and bedrooms.

Color With Confidence

Here are sources that can help you decide on colors for your home. Home improvement stores Ace, Home Depot, and Lowe's have interactive paint selectors. Benjamin Moore and Sherwin Williams have "room painters" online.

Paint a poster board your newly selected color and live with it for a while. You will be able to view the paint in all the different lights that will enter your room and see all its differing colors.

If the whole idea is still scary, consider hiring a designer to help you as well. A design professional can help save you valuable time, limiting choices to those that meet your style preferences and life style needs. It also will help you feel more confident about your choices and prevent you from making mistakes.

Colors to Consider

For the past several years color trends in our homes have been what is

Newspaper Article Example

described as earth tones, colors of nature, or natural, soothing shades. (See, we all use emotions to describe color.) These have been reds, greens, and khakis with accents in gold, and these colors have a lot of warmth.

The trend to use colors from nature will continue, but it is shifting from the warm shades to the cooler shades, with the emphasis on soothing still being the key emotional element. But the switch from warm to cool will not be as drastic as it could be. Even these traditionally cool colors will have undertones of brown to warm them up.

Imagine serene oceanscapes on a slightly overcast day, with shades of blue, green, and lilac gray with a just a touch of pale sunlight coming through, accented with sea oats and sand. Moving forward we will be seeing ocean colors in more homes, not just homes at the beach.

Newsletter

Another way to show your expert status is with a newsletter. A newsletter says you are an expert, someone with an opinion, approachable, current, and knowledgeable, and you strive to find a better way for yourself and your readers. Good newsletters can reach everywhere and repay your time and resources with sales.

The simplest form for small-business owners is the e-mail newsletter or tips. Your e-mail newsletter should, just as in print, provide information and not be just for advertising purposes. You need to offer information that is of value and, in the course of doing that, promote your products and services.

You have to put yourself in your reader's place and think about what you would want to see. A good way to put in appropriate content is to receive input from your readers.

Do not forget to post your newsletter to your Web site. This is another opportunity to attract traffic. You also can promote your newsletter on several sites that list other free newsletters.

Newsletters are part of that crucial constant contact. Anyone that has given you her e-mail, from those who are mildly interested in what you do to those who are your loyal clients, needs to receive your newsletter. Even if you only have five people to send it to, you need to do it.

A newsletter can be as simple as a tip of the month. People do not have a lot of time to read newsletters. Something short that they can use is more beneficial than a long newsletter they do not have time to read.

Newsletter Examples

Short Newsletter Idea:

Tip of the Month: When using plants from outside, create the look of Mother Nature. Do not place the stems into a tight vase. Instead, let them fall as they would in nature.

Long Newsletter:

Mary Larsen Designs and Grow Your Design Biz.com

March 2007

Hello!

Time is flying and things are changing fast — I really should do a better job of keeping in touch and keeping you up with all that is new!

Newsletter Examples

As I mentioned last month — Larsen-Trochlil Designs is now Mary Larsen Designs. I haven't re-launched my current Web site — but I have added a new Web site that features the new name and logo — **www. GrowYourDesignBiz.com.**

There you will see that I am offering classes so you can launch your own design business! It is everything that you will need to get started, and I am so excited to pass on what I have learned so you can get your own dream business started!

 This Wednesday — the 28th — I will be a featured speaker at the Stein Mart at Cary Crossroads for its Spring Boutique Week. I will be sharing tips for your personal design projects and how to shop for accessories for your home. I picked the lunch hour so more of you hopefully can attend— 11:15, 11:45, and 12:15— stop in and join me if you can!

In the meantime, please let me know if there is anything that I can do for you or your friends and family.

Read on!

Redesign and Real Estate Staging Classes

As I mentioned earlier — finally I have launched the training piece of my business. This is for those of you who have asked me in the past to please teach or train others how to get started in the field of redesign, redecorating, and real estate staging — so this is for you!

The first class is the week of April 23 – 27 — and yes! You will learn everything you need to know to launch your own business! The next class is May 14 – 18, and classes continue throughout the year. You will do redesign work in four different homes, as well as learn "the business of the biz."

Newsletter Examples

I am very excited to share what I know and help bring you along to develop your own design business dreams. Click on the link below to see the class details.

Redesign and Real Estate Staging Classes From Mary Larsen Designs

Follow-up to My Extreme Makeover: Home Edition

I hope you all had the chance to see the Riggins family home that aired on *Extreme Makeover* on January 21. I received great notes from over 60 people wishing the family well — and I am quite sure that the Riggins family is pleased with the results.

I was fortunate enough to have the drapes that I designed and constructed actually featured both on the show and on the *Extreme Makeover* Web site! You can see it by cutting and pasting the link below into your Web browser: **http://abc.go.com/primetime/xtremehome/ featuredsears414.html** and enter "the Riggins family"!

The drapes were part of the dressing room castle for the little girl, and it was a really big hit! Click below for the complete story and pictures from the show.

Mary Larsen Featured on *Extreme Makeover: Home Edition* — Full Story

If you know anyone who is thinking about getting into the design business, please send him or her to my Web site, **www.GrowYourDesignBiz.com**. I will be more than happy to talk to him or her and see how my classes can meet his or her needs.

Have a fabulous spring! And as always, let me know if you need anything or if there is anything I can do for you!

Warmest Regards,
-Mary
e-mail: mary@marylarsendesigns.com
phone: 919-773-1445
Web: http://www.MaryLarsenDesigns.com
Feel free to forward this newsletter to a friend.

This kind of contact can prompt people to say, "Oh, that's right. I need Mary to help me with my holiday decorating." They do not have to look for your phone number. In fact, they can just reply to the e-mail.

••⌘••
_____
Mary's Trade Tips

Try your hand as a columnist. Newspapers in your area may look for content. Ask if you can be a weekly or bi-weekly columnist. People send in their decorating questions to the newspaper, and you give them answers. It is not difficult to answer three to four questions per week, and answers are no more than a paragraph. This is a good way to get your name out in the community and be seen as a professional. At the end of each column, write a small blurb about yourself where you can direct people to your Web site.

_____

Using the Media

News Release

Public relations (PR) is all about creating visibility and exposure for your business in the media to encourage sales by communicating with your ideal customers. Public relations does not have to be expensive. A news release is one of the best forms of gaining good PR.

A news release is a brief written summary alerting the local media to your business news and activities. News releases are not only great marketing tools but also far more credible and believable than advertising since they appear to come from an objective third party.

Here are pointers to guide you in writing your news releases:

1. Have a story that is a current event or an issue. A news release should provide enough information to generate interest and just enough to incite people to want to know more. You need to provide good contact information if they wish to follow up.

2. Be the first. If you can report that your business is the first to provide a certain service or that your event is the first of its kind, you should use this information as a news release.

••✣••

Mary's Trade Tips

To have your news release printed on time, send it to the editors at least three to five days in advance. Mailing a release too early is just as bad as mailing it too late because it will be put aside and forgotten. Deadlines do vary depending on the type of media, so be sure and check with the editors in advance.

3. Be unique. How is your service or event different from all the other similar services or events?

4. Target your releases. Targeting your release to specific reporters, news anchors, or programs increases your chances of having the news release published. Additionally, targeting your release will mean that it is placed into it a medium that caters to your specific target market.

You can write a news release for just about anything. Here are examples:

• The opening of your business

- Your first anniversary

- The hiring of a new assistant

- Announcing an article or book that is being published

- A presentation at a particular store

- New services

- National facts that are relevant to your business

Credibility is the one thing that can win the customer's heart. Nothing builds more credibility than a well-written press release that is picked up by the media.

Sample Press Releases

Long Press Release

Mary Larsen to Speak at International Window Coverings Expo

Designer and Business Developer Mary Larsen of Mary Larsen Designs will be speaking at the International Window Coverings Expo in Washington, DC, April 11 – 14, 2007.

March 15, 2007 (PowerHomeBiz), Raleigh, NC – Mary Trochlil Larsen, owner of Mary Larsen Designs, has been selected to speak at The International Window Coverings Expo at Washington, DC, Convention Center April 11 – 14, 2007. She will be speaking on the topics of room redesign and window treatment trunk shows.

The theme of the Expo is CONNECT and features the best that is offered in the window fashion and interior design industries.

"I am honored to be part of the window treatment and interior design Expo," said Larsen. "The Expo is a great opportunity to enhance your business, through cutting-edge industry seminars, dynamic speakers, and educating yourself on the industry's latest trends and products."

If you would like to attend the conference, visit **http://www. windowcoveringexpo.com/**. If you are in the design industry and your

Sample Press Releases

small business is in need of development visit **www. GrowYourDesignBiz.com**.

About Mary Larsen:

Mary Larsen is an established, nationally recognized interior design and decorating professional with a focus on room redesign and window treatments. She is committed to developing design professionals through **www.GrowYourDesignBiz.com** — Designing Your Business, Designing Your Life. Larsen has taught decorating and business courses to women's groups and "trade only" conferences throughout the nation. She has been featured in industry trade publications and is a contributing writer for the *News & Observer* and the *Cary News*.

Mary Larsen can be reached by e-mail at **mary@marylarsendesigns.com**.

Mary Larsen Designs, 3340 Langston Circle, Apex, NC 27539

Contact:

Mary Larsen
Mary Larsen Designs, Inc.
3340 Langston Circle, Apex, NC USA
Voice Phone Number: 919-773-1445
Fax Number: 919-773-0314
Mary@MaryLarsenDesigns.com
www.GrowYourDesignBiz.com
www.MaryLarsenDesigns.com

Short News Release

Apex-based designer Mary Larsen, recently featured on ABC's *Extreme Makeover: Home Edition*, will be offering advice on spring accessorizing at Stein Mart in Cary. Three sessions, entitled "9 Minutes with Mary," are scheduled for Wednesday, March 28, at 11:45 a.m., 12:15 p.m., and 12:45 p.m. at 240 Crossroads Boulevard in Cary.

For information, call Mary Larsen at 773-1445 or e-mail **mary@marylarsendesigns.com**.

Radio and TV

How would you like to be a radio personality? It can be as easy as making a phone call. Advertisements on the radio will be of little value to a redesigner or home stager. Having an interview, however, will get you noticed.

Broadcast Example

There is a local radio station in town, and every Tuesday morning it has a program called "Ask the Expert." People call in and ask questions. The expert gives helpful answers.

After hearing the program, I called the station and told them that I was an expert in interior design, and I would like to be on their show.

They looked at my Web site, saw who I was, checked out my pictures, and decided that I was a professional. They invited me to be on their show. It was that easy.

I was on the show four times within the span of one year. Every single time, I received a call that turned into a client.

This was absolutely free. All I had to do was show up and provide useful information to the listeners.

The same is true for television. Many small towns have local stations that are looking for content. If you see a show that you would like to be on, find something you can say that would be of value to the audience and call the station.

Marketing is about being in front of people. When you are in front of them, they get to know you. Remember, in marketing it is not who you know but who knows you.

Chapter 6

It Is Showtime — Perfect Presentations

$\mathcal{G}$iving a presentation is a great way to put yourself in front of people who are your potential clients. Yet, many redesigners, redecorators, and real estate stagers do not give presentations. The common reasons are:

- I do not know where I should go to give a presentation.

- I do not know what to talk about.

- I have no idea what is involved in giving a presentation.

- I am afraid to speak in public.

In this chapter, we will address these issues and move you beyond them. Knowing how and where to give a presentation can be the single most important way to grow your business.

Finding Your Venue

Finding a venue is not as hard as you might think. The first thing you should do is ask your closest friends what organizations they are in. They are all in something, and some are in many different groups. Ask them what kinds of topics are addressed at their meetings. Also, ask them how often the group meets.

Another place to find a venue is by looking in your local newspaper. The newspaper has a section for community organizations, and it has a contact name listed. Contact that person and ask him what he is looking for.

You should consider the places that you shop, especially when you are shopping for your business. Consider smaller businesses, like paint stores or fabric stores. However, you also can go into larger chain furniture or accessory stores.

Finally, use a search engine, like Google, and search for community organizations in your town.

Possible venues include:

- Networking groups
- Church groups
- Mothers' groups
- Bunco groups
- New neighborhoods
- Realtor offices

- Chamber associations
- Bridge clubs
- Reading book clubs
- Garden clubs
- Civic clubs
- Places you shop

Some groups book their speakers up to a year in advance. Most, however, plan at least four months in advance. This means that, if you want to present in October, you need to be talking to them by June or July. Big lead-time is also important so that you can promote your presentation to others in e-mails, newsletters, and press releases.

> ## *Sample Invitation for Home or Studio Presentation*
>
> You are invited to a fabulous evening of wine and design!
>
> Mary Larsen of Mary Larsen Designs, a full-service interior design firm, will be sharing the latest and greatest in window treatment design. Come for a fun "girls' night out" and hear about the next great trend for your window.
>
> Hosted by:
> Date:
> Time:
> RSVP by:
> Phone:

> ## *Sample E-mail Reminder*
>
> My great friend, Mary Larsen of Mary Larsen Designs, has agreed graciously to come into my home and share her window dressing tips and secrets with my friends and me. Mary was a designer with Christian Dior wedding gowns and now has her own interior design company. Mary's expertise has been featured in many *News & Observer* articles and is sought after by the rich and famous in the Triangle, Atlanta, Charlotte, and Philadelphia areas.
>
> So — mark your calendars for Wednesday, November 19, from 7 p.m. until 10 p.m. I will whip up some fabulous cocktails and hors d'oeuvres and promise a great time with Mary.
>
> Mary will have on site the latest fabric swatches, trims, window designs, blind samples (the Silhouettes are gorgeous!) price lists, etc. If you bring swatches or pictures of the windows you are working on, you can plan the whole thing right in my living room! Mary also can give you on-site estimates

---

Sample E-mail Reminder

or schedule an appointment with you that night. Bring a friend or two — the more the merrier! We should all learn a lot this evening and have fun!

•◆⌘◆•

Mary's Trade Tips

A local department store was having a big Spring Fling. Its theme was "Freshen Your Look." It had fresh new clothes, fresh new make-up, and fresh new home accessories. I called and asked if I could present two topics on freshening up your home. The store was happy to have me.

I spoke on two different topics, creating your home style file and the #1 designer secret for accessorizing your home. I called them "Nine Minutes With Mary." I did each presentation three times over the course of the lunch hour. All it took was a little preparation and one hour of my time.

Although lead-time is important, do not let it stop you from taking a presentation that comes up quickly. If you get the opportunity to present in two weeks, run with it. You do not want to say, "Well, according to my calendar, it takes seven weeks to get ready for and promote a presentation. I do not have that time, so I will not be able to do it."

Tell Them What They Want to Hear

Whatever your topic, your presentation needs to be educational, motivational, and inspirational. When people leave, you want them to know something they did not know before they came that will help them take a step forward. If you do not educate and motivate, you are just entertainment.

As you learn about different venues, who attends, and what the group discusses, you determine if you have something to say that fits in with that group. With most decorating topics, you can get up in front of general women's groups. You also can present in front of businesswomen's groups around the holidays when the focus is on the pleasure of the holidays instead of the crush of business.

Possible topics for a presentation include:

- Does Your Room Need a Doctor?

- Diagnosing Your Room's Ailments

- Addicted to Decorating

- Spring Decorating

- The Power of Placement

- Tips for a Beautiful Room

- The Art of Accessorizing

- Picture-Perfect Picture Placement

- Bring the Outside In

- The Seven Deadly Sins of Decorating

- One-Day Decorating for Busy Moms

It Is All in the Outline

Now it is time to do your presentation. No matter where you present your ideas, following this outline will help you stay organized and give your audience what it wants — to be educated, motivated, and inspired.

Introduction

Start with a short explanation of who you are and why you are able to present this topic to them. This is not a résumé but a short "who I am and why I am here." For 20-minute presentations, your introduction is about one minute long.

Sample Women's Group Presentation Introduction

Thank you all for coming today. When Susan asked me to speak at your women's group today, we wanted to make sure that the topic was relevant to you. Since all of you are small-business owners, your time is valuable, and you definitely do not have a lot of spare time. The last thing you want to do is run from store to store trying to find the perfect decorating items for your home, only to end up with nothing — or worse — the wrong thing, frustrated and out of time!

So today we are going to talk about the #1 designer secret for finding the perfect decor items for your home — fast!

First, I am going to go over with you the things we are going to cover today. I will spend just a minute giving you a bit of my background and then move into …

Sample Home Party Presentation Introduction

Thank you all for coming tonight. When Susan asked me to help her put together a girls' night out, I was thrilled! What could be more fun than getting together with a group of girlfriends to discuss the latest trends in home decor? What a great idea — and a night of "wine and design" was born! So thank you all for being here.

First, I am going to go over with you the things we are going to cover tonight. I will spend just a minute giving you a bit of my background and then move into …

Agenda

Everyone wants to know what you will be speaking about. That is why it is a good idea to give people your agenda. Tell them the topic and the main points you will be hitting upon.

•◆⌘◆•
Mary's Trade Tips

I am doing mini presentations called "Nine Minutes With Mary." In these nine minutes, we are going to cover the "style file" and how to shop for accessories in your home.

The Presentation

Twenty minutes is a typical presentation length. During this time, you will explain your topic and engage your listeners. Remember that they are happy to be there and want to hear what you have to say.

Feedback

Once you have given your presentation, it is time for feedback. You want to know what the audience thought so you can make your next presentation even better. With short presentations in a store, this step may be skipped.

Feedback Example

The Giveaway

People love to get free things. That is why, at the end of a presentation, you always should give away a door prize. To win the prize, they must fill out an entry form.

The form needs to capture their:

- Name
- Telephone number
- Address
- E-mail address

You also can ask if they would like to sign up for your newsletter or if they would like to have you call them for an appointment.

The free giveaway can be anything you want. Door-prize ideas include:

- Decorating magazines, such as *Window Fashions* magazine
- Certificate for your services
- Tassels or trim

It does not have to be anything spectacular; it just has to be free.

The Leave Behind

No matter what kind of presentation you give, you should give the audience something so that they have your information. If the presentation has been planned and promoted and it is on their meeting agenda, leave a folder of information with the group.

Your folder handout can include:

- Simple folder with your business on the cover
- Short biography with your picture

- Color photo page of your *best* work

- Business cards

- Postcards

- Services offered and price list

- An article or press release

- Tips

If you are doing shorter presentations, a postcard is a good leave behind.

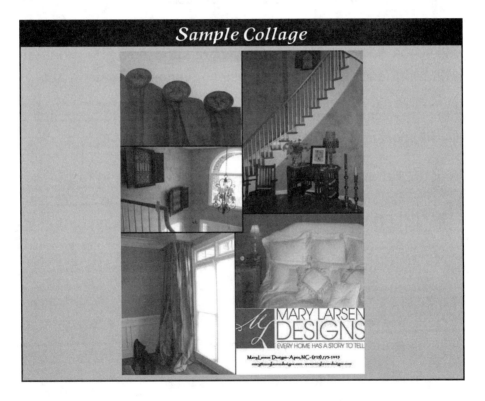

Wrap Up

Do not forget to thank your hostess and present her with a little gift. Then tell your audience to feel free to ask questions.

Be sure to tell them that you have left some forms up front to sign up for a redesign. You might even say, "If anyone wants to sign up tonight, I will give you 25 percent off as a special presentation offer."

When someone has just heard your presentation, she is excited about you and what you do. You regularly will have someone become an immediate client. (See Appendix 5 – 8 for templates.)

Becoming a Public Speaker

The best way to become a public speaker is to start speaking. As you speak on topics on which you are knowledgeable, you will gain confidence. The more practice you have, the easier it gets.

Here are speaking tips to help you on your way to becoming a public speaker:

1. **Eliminate ums.** The best way to do this is to practice talking aloud. When you are driving in the car, instead of listening to the radio, start giving your presentation. You will be surprised at what comes out of your mouth compared to what is in your head. They are different things.

2. **No chewing gum or candy.** Do not have anything in your mouth but your tongue.

3. **Do not pace.**

4. **Empty your pockets to get rid of both noise and bulk.** This also means you should keep your hands out of your pockets.

5. **Maintain the speed of your speech.** When you are

nervous, you are more likely to speed up and become harder to understand. Slow it down and keep it even.

6. **Make eye contact.**

7. **Do not apologize for things that are out of your control.** Do not say things like, "I am so sorry that the light is not coming through the window right so that you can see XYZ." It is not your fault. Do not apologize for things people would not recognize anyway. Do not apologize for not preparing. What you are telling them is that you did not care enough to prepare, and they will wonder why they care to listen.

8. **Avoid rambling.**

9. **No swearing. No joke telling.** Someone will be offended. You do not want to come across as insensitive.

10. **Be clear and enunciate.**

11. **Do not point at people.** People do not like when you do this. If you have to point someone out, do so with an open hand and gesture toward her. If someone asks a question, you may gesture in her direction when you give the answer. It is better to gesture even if you are pointing to something in the room.

12. **Smile.** Even when you are nervous. It is almost impossible to smile too much.

13. **Most important, remember that all these things are forgivable.** If you were entertaining and they got something out of your presentation, they are going to forgive you for any presentation errors.

If you are speaking in front of 500 people, you are not likely to be doing these things or you would not get the job. However, if you are in a home and you are talking to six people, they really do not care as long as you are friendly and educational.

Remember that 10 percent of people watching you will think they can do it better than you can. Just do not worry about them. The other 90 percent are going to love what you do. Work with them.

Once you have started marketing your services, your phone will begin to ring. The next chapter explains how to turn a call into a client.

Chapter 7

From Call to Customer

Listen, Listen, Listen

*W*hen you receive a call from a potential client, you need to be prepared to talk about what you do. During this phone call, you will be asking the questions found on the client contact form and the pre-appointment question form.

•◆✠◆•

Mary's Trade Tips

The biggest asset you have in your business is yourself. Your clients have to trust you. In order to trust, they have to be comfortable. In order to be comfortable, they have to know they can expect the same thing from you. People find comfort in order and consistency.

Start simple. Answer your phone the exact same way every time. If you have hired an assistant, be sure that she also answers the phone the exact same way every time. Your clients will appreciate the consistency, and you will be free to move on and gather the information you need for your client form. Then be sure to add other consistent practices, such as the way you conduct a first meeting with a client. You soon will see that consistent practices free you up to use your creativity.

Before you begin talking about yourself, you need to let clients talk about themselves. When you are providing a service, it is not about you — it is about your client.

When someone calls you, he is likely to say he is interested in redesign and would like you to tell him what you do. This is when it is time to turn the conversation around with questions such as:

- What made you interested in picking up the phone today?

- Have you ever seen any HGTV shows? What is your favorite one?

- Where did you hear about me?

While he answers these questions, he is going to tell you something that is important to him. You will hear words like "frustrated," "sick and tired," and "I cannot do it myself." These are words for you to use later when you explain what you do.

Let the client talk until he has nothing left to say. Once he has told you all about his needs, he has talked himself into working with you and he does not even know what you offer yet. Your questions have helped him understand that not only does he need to have the work done but he needs you to do that work.

When it is clear the client is done speaking, you can say, "Let me explain a little bit about how I work." You will be doing the talking, but you are shaping your talk to what he already has told you.

Perhaps he has said, "I just hate the way my room feels. It is so dark and dreary. In fact, I dread going in there."

In this case, you would start out the conversation like this:

"Redesign is a wonderful way to cheer up, freshen up, and lighten up a room. In fact, once redesigned, the room will become your favorite room in the house."

Then it is time to discuss how you work. Below is a sample script to help you with this conversation. Remember that this is just an example. Over time, you will find the words that work best for you. Additionally, the prices quoted in the script do not reflect what you should charge. Read Chapter 2 to help you determine what prices to charge.

1. We start out every redesign with a $75 consultation in your home that lasts a solid hour. Preferably, this is during daylight hours, since daylight is so crucial to the way you live in a room and to color.

◆◆⌘◆◆
Mary's Trade Tips

Do not wait until the end of your explanation to talk about money. You need to make it clear right up front that you can do what clients need and that it does cost money. You should not hesitate. What you do is of great value.

2. With redesign, unlike interior design, all the decision-making and pressure is removed from you. You will not have to worry about changing your sofa and all the decisions that go along with that choice, like color, the type of foam in the cushions, or whether or not you want piping. Instead, I am going to take my talent to turn the things that you already have and like and make your room the best it can be. There is no risk. If you do not like it everything can be returned to the way it was before.

••✦⌘✦••

Mary's Trade Tips

Relieving the pressure of a traditional interior design project is a huge selling point that redesigners forget to discuss. Let your potential clients know that you have now removed hundreds of decisions that could cause stress.

3. We will go through your home and discuss all the things you are considering doing to achieve the look you want. We can concentrate on just a couple of rooms or do a quick hit of your whole house.

4. After going through your home, we will discuss some ideas on what you can do to achieve your look and feel. Room redesigns start at around $500.

5. At this point, you then decide if you would like to continue to use my services. (At this point, you may want to wait for the customer to comment.)

6. We decide the direction you want to go. This includes your priorities, the look you are trying to achieve, and the investment you will be making. Even if you decide

to go no further, you will get so much information that it will be worth your time.

7. Once approved, a contract will be drawn, and we will establish a 50 percent payment toward the project (Appendix 3).

8. As we move forward, the balance will be due upon completion of the redesign project (Appendix 15).

Avoid This Business Blunder

I had someone call me and say that she watched HGTV all the time and wanted me to come in and do a redesign just like the redesigns she saw on television. My blunder was that I assumed I knew what that meant.

Before listening, listening, listening, I jumped right in and said, "I will come to your home and do a consultation to see the room and determine how the room needs to function for you and your family. Then we will set up the appointment for the actual redesign, which will take about half a day and typically costs around $500, though we will determine that price at the first meeting."

I thought she dropped the phone. Her reply was, "Oh my gosh. It's going to take two appointments, an analysis of the room function, and $500?"

That was the point when I knew I needed to back up. I then asked her what she thought happened when a redesign was done, and she said, "Aren't you just going to move my sofa?"

I had to explain that redesign was a complete process from start to finish, including the reworking of furniture, art, and accessories to best suit the needs of the family. And that is not what she wanted. She only wanted a discussion about furniture placement and some ideas on what accessories to use so she could go shopping. Thank goodness the conversation advanced that far before I showed up for a redesign consultation!

Just because someone has seen the TV shows does not mean they really know what you do. Listen more to his or her needs and problems before jumping in with your solution.

At this point you have addressed every problem and issue that the caller has raised. Now it is time to get an appointment. Try saying, "What is the best time for you to get together with me for this consultation?" Do not say, "Is this something you might want to do?" Go ahead and close positively, as though the caller is already going to make an appointment.

•◆⌘◆•

Mary's Trade Tips

Another way to close is to say, "Which is better for you, Monday at 1 p.m. or Wednesday at 7 p.m.?" Even if both of these times are inconvenient, the caller now is looking at her calendar to find a time that is not. This is known as the positive alternative close.

No matter how much people say they need your help, redesign is not a top priority. They do need and want your help, but it is not likely to be immediate. It can easily take three months from the first time you talked with them until you are done. Everything is more important, even getting groceries. It is just life.

Stagers Armed With Statistics

Selling real estate staging to a potential client is similar to redesign but has distinct differences. A client who wishes to redesign her home wants to find peace and satisfaction in her home. A client who wishes to stage his home wants to sell it quickly and for more money. Since the purpose is different, the sales conversation will be different as well.

Be sure to read the first couple of paragraphs under the heading Listen, Listen, Listen! This applies to any business, including real estate staging.

A home seller may say something like, "I am putting my home on the market, and we have to move as quickly as possible. I am really concerned because there are three other houses in our neighborhood for sale, too. They have been sitting there for more than three months. We just do not have the time for ours to sit that long. I watched one of those HGTV shows that staged a house, and it sold right away."

For this home seller, you will want to explain your process (see below) with the following statistics:

- Home sellers can make at least 3 percent more with home staging. In some areas, that number can go as high as 50 percent.

- Homes that were staged from the outset brought the seller an average equity gain of $16,784.18, according to a study of 300 houses from 2004 to 2006.

- Homes that had not sold in four and a half months after listing sold within a week of being staged by a professional.

- Homes staged before listing were under contract more than twice as fast as comparable homes that had not been professionally staged.

If the home seller is still uncertain, you might consider showing him the math:

Your Mortgage X 4.5 months =
versus
Your Mortgage X 0.25 month =

This is the amount he can save just on his mortgage alone.

For example, if a homeowner's mortgage is $1,000 each month, he will spend at least $4,500 on his home waiting for it to sell if it is not staged (and this is assuming it will sell that quickly). If he stages his home, it could be as little as $250, for a savings of $4,250. Put that way, the seller will see the financial wisdom of staging.

Another way to show those selling a home that they need your services is to compare the process of selling a home to something they already know, such as selling a car.

Expert Example

If you were selling your car, would you get it detailed, clean out the trash, or take it to the car wash? Home staging is doing the same thing to your home. Your home is the biggest investment you have. If you are willing to detail a car, a much smaller investment, imagine how much more effective "detailing" will be when selling your house. Doing so will ensure the biggest return on your investment possible.

If you can get sellers to see their house as a product for sale instead of their home, you have gained a client.

You are also likely to have real estate agents as your clients. Real estate agents also are looking for a quick sale for the most money because it affects their commission. You will want to show the same statistics as you would with a home seller but in a way that discusses their commission.

- Staging costs less than a price reduction and keeps your commission from going down.

- Your listing will stand out because the home will be "move in" beautiful.

- Homes that have been staged sell for more, thus increasing the property values in the entire area.

- When sales are slow, staged homes sell 50 percent faster.

Expert Example

Some real estate agents fear that offering home staging will cut into their commission profits. To help overcome this objection, you can offer the following:

"As the market shifts and homes begin to 'sit on the market,' you need a solution or competitive advantage to offer discouraged home sellers. You need solutions that get their homes sold. That edge is home staging.

"Home staging is a win-win proposition. You may be getting a higher commission, but that means your client will be getting a higher price for his home and get more of his equity."

When talking with the client, be sure to thoroughly explain your process:

1. We start out every real estate staging project with a $125 consultation in your home that lasts a solid hour. Preferably, this is during daylight hours, since daylight is so crucial to the way your home is viewed.

2. We will go through your home, starting at your front door. I will use my real estate evaluation form and discuss with you the things that need to be done for your home to be sales ready. I will capture all these items on the form.

•◆ ⌘ ◆•

Mary's Trade Tips

Let your potential clients know that by working with you to stage their home, they will not have to "guess" at what will have the most impact on their bottom line.

---

3. We will go through your home, room by room, including looking in closets and cabinets. I will discuss with you the things that need to be done and why they need to be done.

4. After going through your home, we will discuss the top five things that will have the most impact on the sale of your home.

5. At this point, you then decide if you would like to continue to use my services. You may want to complete the to-do list yourself, or you may want to work with me to complete the list. (After saying this, wait for the customer to comment.)

6. If we do move forward, a contract will be drawn, and we will establish a 50 percent payment toward the project. The balance will be due upon completion of the project.

Every Season Is a Good Season to Redesign

As your business grows, you will begin to see patterns to your work schedule. This is because people are predictable.

For example, before the holidays, you will find that your business booms. Everything your client has ever wanted to accomplish in her room has to be done before Christmas and the arrival of all the guests. Your phone will start ringing the Monday before Thanksgiving, and you will be busy until the day before Christmas.

Therefore, you need to start talking to people about the holidays in September. Remind them that Thanksgiving is right around the corner. If you are lucky, you may get foresighted people to book early to avoid the rush. For those who wait until the week of Thanksgiving, at least you have planted the seed.

•◆⌘◆•

Mary's Trade Tips

You might think that the holiday season is a difficult time to sell redesign services because people are spending all their money on gifts and will not have money for you. Do not believe it. During this season, everyone is out spending money and writing checks. A business truism to remember is that, if someone already has her checkbook open, it is a lot easier to keep her writing checks. You want to be sure that your name is on one of those checks.

January can be a little slow but only once the bills come in. In early January, people realize that they are not happy with the way their home looked for the holidays. They determine that now would be a good time to change it. They may even make it their New Year's resolution to do something to make their home more enjoyable.

Spring is a good time because people are looking for something new after spending the whole winter indoors.

Summer is steady, but this is one season that there is not a big push since children are out of school.

Back to school is big. Parents look at their house and say, "Oh my gosh. I have got to get this house in order."

These patterns reflect the thinking patterns of people. To capitalize on this, you always need to be assessing what people are thinking about and why.

Expert Example

My first year in business, I really freaked out because the week between Christmas and New Year's Day and the first couple of days of January were totally dead. I was in a panic and worried that I would not have any work for weeks.

Finally, the calls started coming in, and I realized I had not needed to worry. I also realized that the downtime was a great thing. How many jobs have a built in two-week Christmas vacation?

The Style File

Depending on the type of services you offer, you may want to ask your client to create a "style file." This is a collection of magazine pictures that will help you understand her style.

For the style file to be helpful to you and your client, ask her to follow the instructions below. You can send these instructions in the mail or through an e-mail. Once the file is created, the client will be able to refer back to it for her own projects.

> **STEP 1.** Obtain one expandable file folder and a bunch of individual file folders.
>
> **STEP 2.** Label the expandable file folder "My Dream Home." This folder will help identify your likes and dislikes and define your personal style. Are you traditional, modern, contemporary, or eclectic?
>
> **STEP 3.** Label the individual file folders with the rooms in your home — for example, living room, family room, dining room, master bedroom, master bath, guest room, and so on.
>
> **STEP 4.** Take pages out of the magazines in your home, or better yet, buy current home design magazines and use

those pictures. Rip out anything you like and anything that inspires you. However, keep it specific. If you love particular flooring and think it would be great in a kitchen, place that picture in your dream home kitchen folder. If you see window treatments that would look great in your living room, put that picture in your living room file.

STEP 5: You also can take out pages that you dislike. Be sure to mark what it is you dislike and why.

The reason a style file is helpful is because people may not be able to verbalize what they like. They may be able to tell you what they hate, but that is not enough information to help you create a room that they will love.

Your Appearance Matters

First impressions count. Studies about people meeting for the first time reveal that people make decisions about a new acquaintance within the first 30 seconds to two minutes of interaction. This does not give you much time to make a good impression. A professional redesigner who does not take the time to maintain a professional appearance presents the image of not being able to do the job.

When you are making your clothing choice, err on the side of conservative. While it is true that your client knows you are a "creative type," you do not want to shock him with loud colors and unusual styles.

Be sure that you do not wear torn, dirty, or frayed clothing. In addition, refrain from wearing any clothing that has words, terms, or pictures that may be offensive to your client.

Finally, be aware of wearing too much perfume. Not only can the smell be offensive to some; perfume also can cause an allergic reaction.

Being professional is as simple as being at your appointment on time, dressing appropriately, and making a knowledgeable presentation of your abilities.

Meeting the Redesign Room

When you go to the consultation, looking and sounding like the professional you are, you need to remember your digital camera, you notebook and pencil, and your measuring tape. As you go through the different rooms, take copious notes. Note such things as these:

- Colors
- Fabric selection
- Amount of furniture
- Amount of accessories
- Plate stands
- Books

- Any window treatments
- How high the ceilings are
- Any artwork
- Where the entryways are
- Number of lamps available
- Where the windows are

- What rooms are connected to the room that is being redesigned

Once you are in the door and the pleasantries have been exchanged, start the consultation by saying something like this:

"Let's start in the room you wanted me to redesign. I just want you to talk to me about the room. Tell me how you feel about the room. Tell me what direction you think you might want to go.

Tell me how you use the room and which doorways and doors are used the most. Then we are going to go through the whole house and talk about all the different things in your home."

All these things are important to understand. You want to make sure the room can be used in a way that fits your client's life.

──────────── ••⌘•• ────────────
Mary's Trade Tips

Often a room is not used because the furniture is not set up in the room correctly, so the room "feels" bad. Once the room has been re-designed, it turns into an inviting place and is suddenly the favorite room in the house.

───────────

As you are discussing her needs and desires for the room she wishes to have redesigned, your client may start pointing out items in the room that must stay in the room or even stay in the same place in the room. Here is something you can say to help keep these "musts" to a minimum:

"It is not that I cannot work with the things you love. I think it is really important to know what your favorite things are. However, every restriction we put on this room limits what this room can be. If I have the whole house to work from, it is going to be the best that it possibly can be. Every option you limit reduces this. Let's try to keep the limitations to a minimum so you can have the best results. The beauty of redesign is that nothing is permanent. If you do not like it, you can just put it back exactly like it was."

Once you have taken your notes and discussed various options and concerns with your client, it is time to pull out your calendar to pick a redesign date.

•◆⌘◆•

Mary's Trade Tips

You do not want an empty calendar. Make sure that you have some notations on your calendar. You might have a conference call on Tuesday at six that is really your mastermind group and an appointment on the 20th with Janet who happens to be your hairdresser. What those appointments are really does not matter. What matters is that your calendar is not empty.

Additionally, you want to beware of giving your client too many details concerning the hours you choose to work. I know many people work part-time as redesigners, but they are too honest. Their voicemail gives exact dates and times for their office hours. This says to a client that you are not really committed to your work.

If you give specific hours that you will and will not work, a potential client may decide that he cannot fit the redesign into your specific hours and decide to go somewhere else. On the other hand, if you have not told him your hours and he decides he likes you and wants to work with you, he is more likely to fit his schedule to yours, even if he would not have done so initially.

For example, I rarely meet a client for a redesign on Friday. However, not one of my clients has ever heard me say that I do not do redesign work on Fridays. Remember, it is not about you — it is about them.

As you set up your redesign date, your client needs to understand that you will be working in the home while they are gone. The best way to achieve this is to use the magic words "Most of my clients" and "Just like the TV show." You might say something like the following:

"The redesign process is a lot like what you see on the television shows. My clients leave on the day of the redesign. You leave for the day, I rework your rooms, and I call to give you a return time. Then you will come back and see your new room. The best part for you will be the great reveal, and you probably will burst into tears, just like on TV."

•◆⌘◆•

Mary's Trade Tips

Although some redesigners allow their clients to stay in the home while the redesign work is taking place, I tell my clients that they need to be out of the home during the work, until it is time for the big reveal. I compare it to watching someone get ready for a date. No one wants to see you as you curl your hair and shave your legs. You only want him to see you in your heels and pearls. It is the same with your room and redesign.

If you provide shopping services or have items for sale, you will want to let your client know that you may be bringing in some of your own items during the redesign. You can say something like:

"I am going to rework the room with what you have to the best of my abilities. If it is okay with you, I would like to bring some things that will work in your room.

"These things include some lighting, since most homes do not have enough lighting, and some accessories. There is no obligation to buy any of these items.

"When we are done, if there are things that I found really lacking, I will talk with you about those things. If there are things that I pulled from another room, but I know they have to go back because they are necessary in that room, I will talk to you about those things. I will make you a list of items you need to make your room perfect. At that point, you can purchase what I have brought in, hire me to buy those items for you, or take the list I have put together for you and get them on your own."

•◆⌘◆•

Mary's Trade Tips

After setting up the redesign staging date, it is time to grow your business. The best way to grow your business is through client referrals, and the best way to get client referrals is for their friends to see both the room before and after your redesign.

Here is a good way to help your client help you:

"One of the best ways for me to grow my business is when people refer me to other people. The best way for that to happen is for people to see my work. I was hoping that, before the redesign, you could invite friends to come over and see the room. In fact, since you are leaving for the day, you might even bring your friends over that morning, spend the day with them, and bring them back with you when you see the redesign for the first time. Of course, I realize that finding four or five people that can be available for the whole day can be difficult, but even if you could invite just a few of your neighbors the day before, and then again afterwards, I would really appreciate it. They will want to see it, and you will be so pleased with it that you will want to show it off. This is a great thing that you could do for me."

About five days before the redesign, send your client a reminder e-mail that says the same thing. State the date you will be there and the time. Once again, thank the client and let her know that this is the best way for you to grow your business.

Meeting Your Soon-to-Be-Staged Home

The day of your initial real estate staging evaluation has arrived. You come armed with your evaluation form and prepared to have a lot of discussion on why the changes you are suggesting are necessary. Remember, these clients have lived in and loved their home for years. They may need gentle persuasion to let go of their memories and to begin thinking of their home as a product for sale.

Here are things to note as you go through a client's home.

Ask these questions when surveying the exterior:

1. Do the doors, window frames, or fascia need touch-up trim paint?

2. Does the yard need to be fertilized and watered to enhance color?

3. Does the shrubbery need to be cut back?

4. Do seasonal flowers or ground cover need to be added?

5. Do the planting areas need to be weeded and mulched?

6. Are there any missing shutters, gutters, or downspouts?

7. Does yard debris need to be removed?

8. Does the roof need repair, or do broken shingles or tiles need to be replaced?

9. Is the driveway free of excessive cracks or stains?

10. Are fences mended and painted?

11. Is the area in front of the curb and driveway clear of debris?

12. Do the windows need washing?

13. Are there garbage cans, discarded wood scraps, and extra

    building materials around the perimeter of the house?

14. Are patios and decks clear of small items?

Ask these questions when surveying the living areas:

1. Does the room need a deep cleaning?

2. Do the walls need to be repaired or touched up?

3. Do the doors need to be cleaned or touched up?

4. Are the screens in good repair?

5. Does the carpeting need to be cleaned?

6. Do the draperies need to be cleaned?

7. Is the fireplace tile in good condition?

8. Is the fireplace screen in good condition?

9. Is the fireplace hearth clean?

10. Do any doors or windows squeak?

11. Are the closets cluttered?

Ask these questions when surveying the kitchen:

1. Are counters clean and clear of appliances?

2. Does the floor need to be cleaned and waxed?

3. Does the floor need to be replaced?

4. Do the ceiling fan blades need to be cleaned?

5. Does the vent hood need to be cleaned?

Ask these questions when surveying the bathrooms:

1. Does the bathroom need a thorough cleaning?

2. Are there stains in the sinks, toilets, and bathtubs?

3. Does the caulking around the bathtubs and sinks need to be replaced?

4. Are there leaky faucets?

5. Do any drains need to be unclogged?

6. Do the drains need to be sanitized to remove odors?

7. Are the mirrors clean?

Ask these questions when surveying the garage, basement, and attic:

1. Is the garage clear of excess storage items?

2. Does the garage floor have stains?

3. Are there any cobwebs that need to be removed?

4. Are these areas clean and in good repair?

Once you have answered these questions, it is time to create the consultation report. (See Appendix 2.) If your client has hired you only for a consultation, this report will give him the tactics needed to sell his home quickly and for more money. If your client has hired you for a full staging, this report is for you and is a way for you to determine the price of the staging project.

Stick to the List

When you arrive at your consultation, be sure that you follow your checklist so that everything is discussed before the day of the redesign. You want to be sure to discuss the following:

1. Clients will be leaving for the day.

2. You would like them to invite five friends before and after the redesign project.

3. You will be "shopping the house" for items from

other rooms that can be used in the room that is being redesigned.

4. There will be a "holding area" for items that do not get used in the room.

5. You will be bringing in items that they can purchase if they would like to help fill gaps that become apparent as you redesign their room.

6. You will need them to move their own electronics.

Ask the Expert

Q. I did a consultation at someone's home and realized that one entire wall is filled with stereo and television equipment. I do not know how to hook all those items back up. Should I hire someone to come in for me?

A. Although hiring someone to come in is an option, the best answer is to simply state that you do not deal with electronics. Explain that clients will have to dismantle all of it and move it to another room. I will put the TV into the right location during the redesign and then make a note to show them where the rest of the equipment will go.

---

7. You will need them to pick up their room so that you can spend the time redesigning and not cleaning. You can use the words "Most of my clients pick up the room before I arrive."

8. You will ask them if they can have their broom, dust pan, and vacuum cleaner available to you. Let them know that you will not be cleaning their room, but you will be taking care of any messes you have created and freshening up areas that were once covered by large pieces of furniture.

Your plan also contains items behind the scenes, such as follow-up e-mails, sending the style file instructions, date confirmation five days before consultation or redesign, and bringing the appropriate toolkits.

Try to always use the system you have developed for gathering information and discussing details of the redesign or staging with the client. The only time this should vary is during an unusual circumstance. When you do not use your system, you easily may skip something. For instance, if someone sees you in the grocery store and decides to make an appointment for the end of the week, do what you can to force the situation into your normal pattern. You may not have time for a follow-up e-mail. You may realize that your client will not have time to create a full style file.

Since the situation is abnormal, you will be focused on the abnormalities, which may cause you to behave differently. Do not throw the whole list away. Just take out the steps you cannot do, but be sure to follow the other steps. Sticking to the plan will save you frustration in the future.

Confidentiality Is Key

Confidentiality is key to a successful redesign, redecorating, and real estate staging business. The way to keep your client's information confidential is to remember that you can be friendly, but you are not friends. Instead, you have a business relationship.

As you establish a business relationship with your client, you will want to discuss other clients and what you have been able to do for them. However, this needs to be done in a neutral way that does not give specifics.

You might say, "I have a client who ..." without ever saying the client's name. If Suzy referred your new client to you, you may talk about working on her project, but you still will not talk about the relationship you have with her. Talking about the prices you charged or the concerns she had is not appropriate. Nothing will kill your business quicker than talking about another client's money.

There is a big difference between having a good relationship with your client and crossing the line. You have to be able to maintain the fact that you are a professional.

Ask the Expert

Q. I have gotten along with several different potential clients, but after the consultation and telling them what I could do, they did not hire me. What am I doing wrong?

A. The first time I learned this particular lesson involved great enthusiasm on my part. I was so excited about all the things I could do for a client that I really did not narrow the solution down to their need. I just said things like, "Oh, you need a new chair? I can do that!" or "You need built-in bookshelves? I can make that happen!" or "You have beautiful things — I can make this room look gorgeous."

I was not addressing their concerns. They wanted to know, "How does this work? What happens next? How are you going to work with me?"

After a couple of times of being sure that clients and I really hit it off and wondering why they didn't hire me to do the work, it occurred to me: I was not answering their question. When my client said she needed a new chair, after letting her know I could do that, I needed to explain to her how I was going to do that.

In the business process I use, there are several ways to get a new chair from me. After spending time with her and determining how she liked to operate, the answer for her specifically was:

1. I will shop in stores locally that will sell a chair right off the floor.

Ask the Expert

2. I will take digital pictures and be sure dimensions will be correct for the space.

3. You then will decide which chairs you want to see so you can sit on them.

4. You can do that alone, or you can hire me to join you.

5. You can purchase the chair directly from the store and have it delivered.

It did not matter that I carry exclusive furniture lines that she could purchase only through a designer. It did not matter that fabric samples and furniture could be viewed online, and the chair could be custom designed and ordered and delivered in 12 weeks. It did not matter because that is not what my client needed.

It was up to me to determine which one of my services would best suit her needs. A custom piece of furniture that would take her 12 weeks to receive and she would never see in any of the homes of her friends was not what she was looking for at this time.

Being the creative types that we are and knowing what we know about our business, it is easy to answer this question by saying, "Any way you want. We can do anything that you want."

The problem is that your client does not know what she wants. She may think she knows, but once you start asking her questions and letting her know what services you offer, her wants may change dramatically. Determining what the client is looking for is one of the toughest parts of your job.

Many clients know they need something, but they may not be sure what that something is. Telling them that you can do anything they want does not help clarify the situation for the client. "Anything" is just too broad. It does not let the client know how you will do things for them specifically, and ultimately, that is the answer they are looking for.

Consider these things before answering this question:

Ask the Expert

First, your answer must be suited to the specific client and her needs. Be sure that you are clear on what the client is looking for. If not, ask questions until both you and the client are clear.

Now that you are clear on just what it is your client wants, you need to consider the services you offer and be sure to tailor these services to the client's needs. Now I know that sounds simplistic, but this too is important. How can you satisfy the wants of this client? How are you going to do this? How does this work?

Being vague or overly broad with your response will not move you forward in your design work. When you are unclear, so is your client. This eventually will lead to discomfort, which eventually will lead to lack of trust — and trust is the most important element in your relationship.

You now have your first client. Before arriving, be sure you know the concepts and use the tips in the next chapter.

Chapter 8

It Is Not What You Have but Where You Put It

Your Creative Purpose

Redesign is more than just aesthetic beauty. Beauty is a surface thing that does not equate into peaceful surroundings. For example, you may have a beautiful chair and sofa, but they are not in the right place in the room, and therefore the room "feels" bad. You have beauty but not peace.

A warm, inviting, and peaceful atmosphere can be created in any home or office simply by applying the principles of redesign. Using your client's existing furniture, art, and accessories, redesign will define the space, create intimacy, and enhance the flow of the rooms, one to another.

Redesign looks at the process of redefining the spaces in a home based on the life style of the client. As you redesign your client's room, you will help her move furniture and accessories, sometimes from one room to another, making the room the best it can be.

before

after

Instead of a surface beauty, you will create a deep peace. When your client's redesign is completed, she will have a new appreciation for her home and her furnishings. Her rooms will be focused, balanced, and beautiful. They will give your client an inner sense of well-being.

Home staging is the art of preparing a home for sale using the skills of cleaning, decluttering, depersonalizing, and redesigning. Home staging used to be just the advice to clean up and declutter. As a professional stager, you know that staging is far more. You have to create the right atmosphere.

When it comes to sales, first impressions are everything. A potential home buyer will decide to enter a home based on the outside appearance. And once inside, he makes up his mind about a home within about ten seconds. This means that you have ten seconds to create an atmosphere that entices the imagination and creates a longing in the buyer.

Therefore, your job is not only to help your client declutter but also to help her create a clutter-free environment. Your creative abilities will help you determine what items to remove and what items to rearrange. Your knowledge will help your client improve her home's curb appeal.

For home staging, begin with the basics of redesign to learn more about the elements of the room. Then see the section Home Staging Differences at the end of this chapter for more specifics on home staging.

Psychology of Color

Studies have shown that, next to smell, color has the greatest impact on the emotions. Because of this, people are afraid of color. The emotions that color brings to an individual are so strong that it seems easier to stay neutral than to try color. Your client will not be able to articulate it in this way but will say something like, "I am afraid I am going to make a mistake, and the room will look horrible."

Therefore, as you redesign a client's room, you need to be aware of his color preferences and how those colors affect him. It does not matter if the "hot" colors are brown and pink. If he does not emotionally like those colors or he reacts poorly to them, they are not going to make your client's home feel the best it can be. Just because it is a trend does not mean you need to follow it.

One of the best ways to find out what colors appeal to the client, beyond looking at his style file and asking him to tell you color preferences, is to look in his closet. The color you see the most is the color that appeals to him.

There can be limitations to color because of trends. Homes follow fashion and are two years behind what you see on the runway. You may find that the color your client loves is not available in furniture or accessories because it is not currently in style. In this case, you can use neutral colors and add your client's favorite hues with paint.

••◆⌘◆••

Mary's Trade Tips

If someone tells me that they like sage green, I ask him to point out the color using a color palette or from the photos in their style file. Sage green to one person is not the same sage green to another. This is true with any color. Use tangible items such as paint swatches or photos when working with colors, not words.

before

after

•◆⌘◆•
Mary's Trade Tips

If you do not like the way a color looks in a paint can, you are not going to like it on the wall. A salesperson may say that it will look different on a wall, and it may, but it is not going to change that much. If you do not like what you see in the can, do not bother to take it home.

Do you plan to offer color consultations or painting as add-on services? You may want to keep the following in mind:

- Dark colors can make a room feel cozy.

- Use color to show off architectural elements.

- Flat finishes help hide imperfections in a wall.

- Painting the walls and ceilings the same color makes the room look bigger.

- A ceiling painted a shade or two darker than the wall will make the ceiling feel lower.

- A ceiling painted a shade or two lighter than the wall will make the ceiling feel higher.

- Using light, cool colors, such as blue and green, make a room seem larger.

- Using dark, warm colors, such as red and yellow, make a room seem smaller.

Before your redesign or staging project, you will have discussed color with your client and should have a good idea what she wants and needs. Ignoring her emotional connections to color will be disastrous.

Psychology of the Eye

In addition to the concern with color, you also will need to be aware of the way the eye moves around a room. Through studies of the eye, researchers have found patterns that the eye uses to take in its surroundings. These patterns will have a direct impact on how you redesign a room.

For instance, if you are right-handed, your eye automatically will be drawn to the right-hand corner of the room and then to the center and then will read the room from left to right — just the way the eye reads a book. If someone is left-handed, her eye will go to the left-hand corner of the room first, then to the center, and then back to read it like a book. Since only 10 percent of the population is left-handed, your focus should stay on the right corner.

If you stand in the most used doorway of a room and look to the right-hand corner, you will find one particular item — the television. Having a television in the room is not a problem, but having it as the first thing a person sees may be. As a designer, you will not want this to happen since a TV is just a black hole. No one really wants to see a black hole when he walks into a room. When you place the television, keep that in mind.

In addition to reading a room left to right, the eye also goes through the room from high to low and back again. The pattern is similar to an inverted, undulating S curve, starting high on the left, moving lower, then up, and then lower until it finally goes up again at the right.

Finally, the eye searches for a place to rest. Not every spot on every wall needs decoration. The eye needs to have a place to stop so it can appreciate what is in the room. There is such thing as good white space.

Think about the noise of a crowded room. Everyone is talking, but you cannot really hear what anyone is saying because too much is going on. The same thing happens in an overly decorated room. The eye can see all the colors and patterns but cannot appreciate any of them because of all the clutter.

Now that you are aware of emotionally charged colors and the movements of the eye, it is time to move on to some basic room principles.

Room Basics

Almost all rooms — no matter what the home or where it is located — can be reduced to five basic shapes:

- The square room
- The bowling alley room
- The rectangle room
- The L-shaped room
- The room with pre-existing angle

Knowing this will make your job easier. It means that once you have worked in a room and have determined what works best, every time you are in a room that is of that basic shape, the placement of furniture basically will be the same. What works well in a bowling alley room virtually always works well in a bowling alley room. Knowing this will give you confidence as you move from home to home. You will not have to feel anxious wondering what you are going to do since you have worked in a bowling alley room before.

Here are a few high-level tips to use when considering the arrangement of any room:

- **First impressions.** If the view from a doorway is the backs of chairs or the sides of wooden furniture, the room will feel uninviting. The same is true for rows of furniture pushed against the walls. Angled groups, on the other hand, look cozy.

- **Convenience.** You want the room to look as wonderful as possible. However, if the room cannot perform its function adequately, you have not done your job.

- **Traffic.** Consider the most frequently used items in a room and the ease of access to them. In a kitchen, this principle is known as the "golden triangle" and determines where to place the oven and refrigerator in relation to the sink. The TV, sofa, door, and fireplace can create similar traffic paths in a living room.

before

after

Location, Location, Location

Nothing makes more of an impact on a room than the placement of the furniture and accessories. While in business, you are going to see rooms filled with beautiful individual items, yet the arrangement, and therefore the overall feel, diminishes these elements. You also will see rooms filled with dated and ugly furniture and accessories, and with the help of your correct placement, they will end up looking amazingly good.

The key to a successful room is achieving a sense of balance and proportion with furniture and accessories. Your goal is to create a room that feels harmonious, balanced, and connected. The secret is to work with the pre-existing planes, lines, and angles of the space and your items to create your great look. The following tips will help you achieve this goal.

••⌘••
_____

Mary's Trade Tips

It is not what you have — it is where you put it.

_____

Reading the Room

You read a room much like you read a book, with your eyes moving from left to right. Keep your eye moving smoothly around the room by creating highs and lows, much like an undulating wave or the shape of an S curve on its side. Use accessories, artwork, and window treatments to help build the highs and lows.

Let Shapes Lead You

Use the shapes of the room and the shapes of the items in the room to help guide you in your design process. For example, an angle built into a room, such as a fireplace built into a corner, dictates that you place a piece of furniture in the room on a corresponding angle in order to achieve a sense of balance so the room can "feel" right.

Like With Like

Similar shapes work best when they are together. If you have a short wall and a tall wall, typically your short furniture piece will go on your short wall, and your tall furniture will go on your tall wall. This also works with a horizontal piece of art over a long sofa or using small accessories in a small room and large accessories in a large room. Think tall with tall, small with small, narrow with narrow, wide with wide.

Be a Groupie

"Like with like" applies to collections as well. You want to group collections and similar items together, not spread out all around the room. Your collection will have much more impact when all the pieces are displayed together. This actually allows someone to stop and view it all as one and appreciate it in full. When it is all spread out, the collection is diluted, and it is very easy to miss important pieces.

Grouping applies to even small collections, such as framed photos. You will get much more impact with three framed photos sitting next to each other than with those same three photos spread throughout the room.

Too Much of a Good Thing

As you work on putting like things with like things, do not go overboard. If you have a wall with three doors in it and two tall windows, placing an armoire on that wall that is virtually of the same shape will just be too much. Try to break up the hard lines of the doors and windows with shaped draperies and strategically placed artwork to help move the eye up and down.

Hard and Soft

When placing furniture in a living or family room, try to alternate hard pieces, such as tables and armoires, with soft pieces, such as upholstered chairs and ottomans. Too many hard pieces together will make the room feel hard. If hard pieces must be placed next to each other, greenery and plants can be used to soften the edges.

What Is That Up There?

Your room is not just your four walls — it contains the ceiling too. Do not forget to relate the room to what is going on in the ceiling, such as beams or vaulting.

Magic Number Three and the Pleasing Triangle

When placing accessories and lighting, your eye likes sets of three. That is why so many accessories you can buy today already come in a set of three. And just like three, your eye likes triangles. You will see this in shapes with high, medium, and low, as well as in lighting, having three points that can create the shape of a triangle throughout the room.

The Booster Book

To help achieve those groupings of three at high, medium, and low levels, use a good book. These various levels create interest — books without jackets always work well to create the varying heights. Check out your local thrift store for good solid books with black bindings that can work in any room.

The Energy of Angles

Placing furniture on an angle in a square room instantly will add energy and movement to a room. Be sure to consider the functionality of the room — for example, you might not want your daughter's bedroom to have more "energy" when you are trying to get her to sleep.

Expect the Unexpected

Be sure to use your creativity when designing your room. Follow the guidelines, but do not get trapped by rules. What you want to hear from your client is "I never would have thought of that!" That is the value you bring. Consider moving a dining room buffet into the living room to be used as a dry bar. Or put your client's small collection of fortune cookie fortunes all together under glass in a frame.

before

after

The Friendly Family Room

Most family rooms focus on the television, and there really is not much "family" going on at all. Help your family reconnect by creating seating areas within an eight- or nine-foot radius, putting your family members in close proximity. This grouping should be able to accommodate up to six people, and you may find your family actually talking to each other.

For important seating areas, such as those between a husband and a wife, aim for the seats to be within three or four feet of each other. This close arrangement actually will encourage conversation.

A Room With a View

When you have completed arranging the furniture in your room, be sure to sit in every available seat and view the room from all angles. This may help you with finishing touches, as well as allow you to see what every guest in the room will see.

Once the furniture and accessories are in their proper places, it is time to hang the artwork.

Picture-Perfect Picture Placement

It is much easier to place artwork after the other elements of a room have been placed, such as furniture and light fixtures. Having these objects placed first will help dictate the location of your artwork. Remember, almost anything and everything can be hung on a wall and framed.

Consider who you are and the story you are trying to tell. Artwork in a traditional setting is symmetrical, and a cozy feeling can be established with close groupings. Contemporary pieces hang alone for a sleek, finished feel. What look and feel are you trying to achieve?

Here are tips that can help you hang artwork with a designer's eye.

Consider Spacing

Try putting artwork closer together rather than farther apart. You can determine the amount of space needed between pictures by taking a cue from the width of the frame. You may even want to hang the pictures so that the frames are touching.

Eye Level

What is eye level? Rarely are you going to find a home where all the people who live there and all the guests who visit are the same height. Therefore, there is really no such thing as eye level. Rather than eye level, consider the wall and its surroundings. If you have a spot in the living room that always is used for reading, consider placing a picture where you can see it easily while relaxing with a good book.

Relate

When working with a group of pictures, try to relate them in some manner. For example:

- All black-and-whites or all color photos
- All framed in the same size and style frame, regardless of the size of the picture
- All framed in the same color frame

This relation will help unify the group.

Proportion

Always consider balance, scale, harmony, symmetry, and asymmetrical arrangements.

Now let us look at principles specific to home staging.

Home Staging Differences

Home staging works for all properties regardless of the price point because home staging is about preparing a home for a faster and more profitable sale and marketing a property to the most potential buyers for its target audience. Homes ranging in price from $100,000 to $10 million sell faster and for top dollar compared with the competitors in their price range.

The focus of staging is to make a home more marketable by creating the most appealing home to the greatest number of prospective buyers. It should be impersonal enough not to infringe on a buyer's own sense of style. Although your client's personality needs to be removed, the personality of the house still needs to come through.

In addition to the redesigning tips already mentioned, you will want to focus on cleanliness, decluttering, and curb appeal.

Let us look at some tips in each of these areas.

Cleanliness

- Wash windows inside and out
- Clean out cobwebs
- Re-caulk tubs, showers, and sinks
- Polish chrome faucets and mirrors
- Clean out the refrigerator
- Wax floors
- Dust furniture, ceiling fan blades, and light fixtures
- Bleach dingy grout
- Replace worn rugs
- Hang up fresh towels

- Clean and air out any musty smelling areas

Decluttering

- Remove two-thirds of the books from bookcases
- Pack up knickknacks
- Clean off everything on kitchen counters
- Clean out the closets
- Pack up two-thirds of items in kitchen cabinets and drawers so they appear spacious
- Put essential items used daily in a small box that can be stored in a closet when not in use

Curb Appeal

- Paint the front door
- Buy a new welcome mat
- Shine the front door handle and knocker
- Add flowers to the front porch for color
- Put landscaping items, such as water hoses and garbage cans, out of sight

Staging Vacant Homes

There will be times when you are asked to stage homes that are vacant. This occurs when an owner has moved already and when you stage model homes. To stage vacant homes, you will need to have furniture and accessories.

If you choose this avenue of staging, there are two ways to go about it.

First, you could buy what you need to make the home show well.

These items would be kept as part of your staging supplies. To keep the costs affordable, buy items that will be the most versatile for your home staging business. Consider it part of the startup costs that will add value to your service down the road.

Avoid This Business Blunder

Using furniture you have purchased to stage homes can be effective, depending on your particular niche market. Using smelly furniture is not.

The big home staging day arrives, and you head off to your storage unit, open the large door, and … what is that smell? The upholstered furniture smells musty. There is no way you can put this furniture into your client's home, and you have no time to clean it or rent new furniture.

Do not let this happen to you. If you store your furniture in a storage unit, you can combat these odors with products such as Febreeze. Other ways to keep the musty odors and dusty surfaces at bay are to:

- Use a climate-controlled storage facility

- Cover large pieces of furniture with sheets

- Place small props in plastic storage bins

Your other option is to use a furniture rental company. Have the rental company drop off and pick up the furniture at the home you are staging.

• ◆ ⌘ ◆ •

Mary's Trade Tips

Rather than list rented items separately on an invoice, which ends up looking pricey, list "accessories and furnishings" with a fee for the whole package.

Providing furnishings is a great service for your home staging clients since buyers have trouble picturing an empty home furnished. When you stage houses that are vacant, you are showing them how comfortable and homey it can be.

As you get started, you may want to consider staging vacant homes with vignettes. A vignette is a small arrangement of furniture in each room, giving the room purpose and allowing the clients to see room proportion and flow.

Expert Example

- Set up a small bistro set in the kitchen or breakfast nook. Set the table as "tea for two."

- Put pretty towels in the bathroom with a luxurious basket of bath items.

- Put some fruit or flowers on the kitchen counter.

- Place an air mattress on boxes with beautiful bedding in the master bedroom.

- Place a beautiful book on the bed with a nice pair of reading glasses.

Staging houses with vignettes is a great time to really get creative. Make sure you appeal to a wide range of buyers and portray an enviable life style. Your staged homes will outshine all the others in your buyer's eyes.

With your design knowledge in hand, it is time to redesign!

Chapter 9

A Day in the Life Of...

A Day in the Life of ... reveals the details of a redesigner's day with information crossing both the redesigner and home stager line. Although the redesigning day and the home staging day are not exact, many of the same principles apply.

For more ideas on what takes place on the day of a real estate staging evaluation, see Chapter 7 and the real estate staging evaluation form in Appendix 2. For a comprehensive look at the many things that can be done to stage a home, please see Teri B. Clark's book, *301 Simple Things You Can Do to Sell Your Home NOW and For More Money Than You Thought.*

Arrival and Send-Off

The big day of your redesign project has arrived. You come in with your toolkit and a smile on your face. The smile is necessary because even though your client is excited about the changes, he also may be a bit apprehensive.

••⌘••

Mary's Trade Tips

Take your shoes off at the door each time you go outside to haul something in. Your client does not want the dirt from outside coming inside. Remember, you are working as a laborer in his home.

Keep this thought in mind as the project moves forward, as well. For instance, do not stand on a client's furniture, drag furniture across hardwood floors creating scratches, or carelessly move furniture. Then, whatever mess you make, clean it up.

On the day of the consultation, though you explained the process to them, this is a wonderful time to remind your clients of key points. One is the holding area. You want to be sure that your client is aware that there will be items that will need a new home and that you will not be the one to find that new home.

You can explain the holding area this way:

"As you know, I will be using things from other rooms. Some things that are currently in the redesigned room will no longer have a home when I am finished. These items will be placed in what I call the 'holding area.' The redesigned room will look great. Your dining room, however, which has been designated the holding area, may have a couple of lamps, some accessories, and maybe even a small piece of furniture in it that will need a new home."

Remind them what time you expect to be finished and be sure you have the correct phone number so that you can call them about an hour before you finish. Then it is time to send them on their way.

Take "Before" Pictures

"A picture speaks a thousand words," and you want to document every job you do with "before and after" pictures to show future clients. These photos will be all you need to sell your next redesign.

Take your photos by starting in one corner of the room and working your way around the room, getting a picture from every angle. Keep in mind that the finished room will have completely different focal points, so every angle of the room, no matter how bare or boring, needs to be photographed.

Remove It All

No matter how many times you have redesigned a room, you need to empty the entire room. You may believe that you know the right place for all the large pieces of furniture, but you may not really know the perfect placement of the furniture if you do not empty the room to allow yourself to see it.

As you empty the room, you will group the items in another room — the holding area — placing like items with like items. For example, group the following:

- Furniture
- Lighting
- Accessories
- Wall hangings

••⌘••
___

Mary's Trade Tips

If the largest piece of furniture is too big to move out, move it into the center of the room.

___

Reverse the Process

Once you have all the furniture out, it is time to reverse the process and put it all back in again.

Furniture First

As you are placing the furniture, you have to pay attention to the architecture. Be aware of the shape of the room and the permanent features like windows, walkways, doorways, and fireplaces.

Another architectural feature is the angle. If there are any angles in a room, you have to incorporate them. For instance, you may have a fireplace or flooring on an angle. Perhaps it is a half wall with a slanted ceiling. No matter where you find the angle, you cannot ignore it. Something else in the room will need to go at an angle or the whole room will feel wrong.

••⌘••
___

Mary's Trade Tips

There is a "new" architectural feature that you will have to overcome — the wall-mounted TV. People put it where they think it works. Sometimes it does not work where it is. When it does not, I pretend it is not there. After I determine the best place for it, I let clients know where that is, and then they handle removing it and putting it in the right place later.

___

Once you have identified the architectural features, it is time to determine your focal points. In some instances, one of the architectural features can be a focal point, as in the case of a fireplace. If there is not a focal point, you will need to create one. The focal point will help you place seating. You also may run into the problem of having to address two to three focal points, such as a beautiful view, a fireplace, and a television.

Now that you know the focal point, it is time to start moving the furniture around. Begin with the biggest piece, which is typically the sofa, and have it face the focal point for your first try.

Do not limit yourself when considering the placement of the sofa. If you believe you know where it goes, you have about an 80 percent chance of being correct. If you do not try it in different places, however, you may miss the 20 percent chance of finding a better place than you originally envisioned you would find. The process can show you something you were not expecting.

When you are done, you can say to your client that there is no better placement for the sofa. In fact, you can tell her that there is no reason to rearrange this room because you have found the best arrangement for the furniture they have.

Once you have the largest piece of furniture placed, working down in size, you will bring in all the upholstered and hard pieces. No matter what, you place all the furniture before you do anything else.

•◆⌘◆•
Mary's Trade Tips

Do not let the wrong thing dictate the right thing. If you know that you are going to have a sofa in the living room, it does not mean that the matching armchair has to fit in as well. So place the sofa in the best place, not thinking about if the armchair will work.

This is a good time to "shop" the house and consider other furniture you might bring in. Perhaps there is a fabulous little chair in the guest room or a unique side table in the dining room. These pieces will help you bring the most to the room you are redesigning.

The hardest part about the entire redesign job is the need to ignore color. You have to reduce things to shape. Your client might have the perfect sofa but in the wrong color. If you do not use it because of the color, the rest of the room is going to be wrong. For someone who is visual, like a redesigner, color is difficult to let go of. Keep in mind that a badly colored sofa in the right spot is better than no sofa or the wrong shaped sofa in the right spot.

Expert Example

During one consultation, my client informed me that she did not use her front door. Instead, everyone came in the back door. The reason was obvious — the front door was not functional because of all the furniture in the way.

When I redesigned the room, I was able to open up the area in front of the door, allowing the coat closet to be used. Additionally, I used furniture to create a walkway into the living room without taking up precious floor space.

Now my client has a beautiful living room and a functional front door. Instead of guests coming in the back door into a kitchen full of dirty dishes, they now come in the front door into a comfortable and peaceful living room.

Area Rugs and Lighting

After placing the furniture, you will place any area rugs you plan to use in the room. Area rugs need to make sense with the placement of the furniture. More often than not, the widest part of an area rug will parallel the front of the sofa, with the front feet of the sofa anchored on the rug.

After the rugs are placed, it is time to look at the lighting. Nine times out of ten, people do not have enough lighting. You may find that the two lamps in the living room are the only two you can use. Hopefully you noticed this on the consultation, and you have come prepared with extra lighting that the client can purchase. If you do not have enough lighting, you will need to make a note that they will need a lamp in that spot and give them a specific size.

There should be a minimum of three lighting elements in the room. Ideally, this lighting will create a triangle shape when it is placed. Be sure to also consider high, medium, and low lighting in regard to the height of the room.

Wall Hangings

When you begin to hang the artwork, start with the focal wall and work to the right. You need to complete a wall before moving on. Do not hang something on one wall and then something on another. It is better to have three finished walls and a blank wall than to have four walls that are almost done.

Once again, you may need to reduce wall hangings to shape. If you have the perfectly sized painting but it has the wrong colors or wrong scene, hang it on the wall anyway. This will help your client visualize what they need to fill the spot. Remember, you do not want your artwork to hang at the same level throughout the room, creating a straight line.

Accessories

The entire time you have been placing all the other items, you have had to resist the urge to start accessorizing. Now you can finally bring out those accessory items, starting with any tall plants or trees — they are practically pieces of furniture.

As you did with the artwork, start accessorizing with the focal wall and work to the right. You need to complete a wall before moving on. Do not jump around the room. It is better to have three finished areas and an empty area than to have a room full of "almost done."

When you place accessories, you want to put like with like. For instance, if your client has a collection of fish, you need to keep her fish as a collection. This allows for impact. Do not place the fish all over the house — this loses impact, and you may not even notice that there is a collection of fish. At best, someone will see it and think, "Wow. They sure do have a lot of fish everywhere." The response you are going for is, "Wow. They sure have a nice fish collection."

For more decorating tips see page 175, titled Location, Location, Location.

Expert Example

I redesigned a large great room of a country home. This room had a little single doorway to the kitchen, a huge sliding glass door, and a doorway into the front room. The front door opened directly into this little front room.

The client spent all his time watching TV in the great room, and nothing ever happened in that little front room. In fact, my clients assumed that it was a dining room since it had a doorway into the kitchen. They had placed a large dining room table there but never ate there. Those who came to the front door virtually fell into this dining room and then had to squeeze by the large table and chairs to get to the great room. It was an unusual situation.

The great room was huge. It had sliding glass doors, a big fireplace, and a staircase that led up to a loft. The sliding glass doors led out onto a deck, overlooking a beautiful view of a lake.

The client told me that he always used the great room. He loved the view of the lake and loved all the windows that made the room feel so bright. This was the room his family lived in, and he wanted it to be both beautiful and functional.

Expert Example

I had my work cut out for me.

I took the dining room furniture and moved it into the great room diagonally in a corner by a double window. Now, instead of eating in their tiny kitchen, the family could eat at their previously unused dining room table while enjoying the incredible view.

Next, I used the fireplace as a focal point and created conversation areas.

In the front room that formerly had been used as the dining room, I moved two comfy chairs, the television, and some small tables. This room was now a cozy spot to watch television or read or just sit and talk. When guests came in the front door, they walked into a welcoming spot where they could sit down and chat.

The great room now was focused on the outside view and allowed for dining and visiting. The entire downstairs now was being used instead of just the sofa and the television in the great room.

Take "After" Pictures

Before bringing your client in to see her new room, be sure to capture the "after" pictures you need. It will be so hard to get these pictures once your client is home, so get them before the client arrives. Start in the same place as you did for the "before" pictures and work your way around the room, being sure to take the pictures from the exact same spot.

Take Note

At this point, it is time to write down any information you want to pass on to the client. For example, you may note that the fish painting you used is the right size but really should be switched out for something in that size with a different color combination. This information will be a great way to share with your client the different additional services you may want to provide for them.

The Reveal

You have taken everything out of the room and put everything back in again. You have cleaned up the mess. You have written down any details the client will need to know concerning the redesign. Now it is time to bring her in for the big reveal.

When she arrives, you need to prepare her for what she is going to see.

"You are going to love your new room, but it may take a moment to get used to it. Change can be a bit difficult, but I know you are going to be delighted." Then you step back and keep your mouth shut. Listen to what she has to say so that you can play up those things when it is your turn to talk.

•◆⌘◆•

Mary's Trade Tips

I want to be there for every client reveal. I bring clients in with their eyes closed, just as they do on the TV shows. I want to see them so excited that they are dancing around and hugging everyone in the room and when they start crying because they are so happy.

Expert Example

One of my favorite reveals was with a woman who was reserved. We were doing a pure redesign, bringing in no new items. While working with her, I realized that she was not prone to excitability. She did not use words like "I love it" or "It is the best thing ever." In fact, she was not even that interested in the work – her daughter had arranged the redesign. She told me that her home was just a place to sleep and nothing much more than that.

As with all my other clients, at the time of the reveal, she had her eyes closed, and then I introduced her to her new room. There was stunned silence. The look on her face was one of complete awe. And then she started talking.

She said things like, "Where did you find this table? It is beautiful!" and "I never liked my window treatments, but now they really showcase my gorgeous sofa," and "This artwork was never seen in the other room, and now it looks like it was commissioned specifically for this room!"

Then she turned to me, with tears in her eyes, and said, "Thank you so much for making me feel good about the things that I have purchased and loved. I had become discouraged and had begun to doubt that I had any taste. Now I know that I just needed an expert to help them work together!"

And yes, we booked another redesign job for another room in the house.

Let Them Know What Else You Offer

When your client comes home for the reveal, you already will have a list together of items she needs to make her room perfect. Here is one way to discuss those missing items:

"I have put this list together for you, and I will be happy to go get these items for you, or you can take this list and get the things yourself. You are welcome to buy the things that are already in your room, as well. Live with them for a day, and if you do not want them, I can come back tomorrow and pick them up."

Then it is time to talk to the client about add-on services. Depending on what services you offer, you can say something like:

"I see you do not have any window treatments in your house. I have a partner who does window treatments, and I would be happy to have him come in. He would be able to make something really awesome for this room."

Or

"I am glad you love it. When the holidays roll around, if you do not like to decorate, give me a call. I love to decorate homes, and it will take the pressure off you. If I can do what I have done with this room, imagine what I could do with all your Christmas things."

Or

"We put the whole room together, and it looks really great. Nevertheless, you might have noticed that the sofa is still blue, and nothing else in this room is. As you said before the redesign, you knew you were going to need a new sofa. I will be glad to help you with that. You may need a new paint color palette, too. That is something I can help you select as well."

Your add-on services should flow naturally based on what you have done for clients and will tell them how you can make their room or home look even better.

Avoid This Business Blunder

One of my clients found and hired me after reading several articles I had written for our local newspaper. She said she enjoyed my writing and felt that the things I had to say about design made a lot of sense to her.

We started working together, and she made it clear that she was a hands-on person. She wanted to decorate on her own and use me as a consultant to help validate and confirm her decisions while working her way through her projects. Or so I thought.

We spent several months working together – she would explore options for decorating, and we would meet and discuss the things she had done and what she wanted to do next. I gave guidance to her projects and pointed out things that were working well and other things that I thought might be getting off track of the overall design concept.

After several months our appointments grew farther and farther apart and eventually tapered off all together. The relationship ended amicably enough; I would run into her on occasion around town, and we always had pleasant conversations. But sometime later I learned she had hired another designer. And not only that, but they had done tons of new and exciting things in her home, like painted ceilings with a faux finish and custom window treatments with tons of embellishments!

Avoid This Business Blunder

I was confused. I was so sure that I had done exactly as my client wanted – I had guided her through her projects and kept her from going wrong. Isn't that just what she asked for? Well, apparently not. Somewhere along the line – whether she was aware of it or not – she wanted more design help than just guidance. She wanted someone not only to guide her project but to lead the project — to take her ideas and grow them into new ideas, which she wanted to have done for her, rather than doing herself.

If there was one thing I was not doing, it was suggesting new and different services that I offer. I could not even remember the last time I had suggested a service to her that was in the design project but beyond her own hands-on approach. If I occasionally had suggested to her other services that I offer, I could have given her the opportunity to let me help her more than I already was. And because I did not, she found someone else who would.

Shopping Add-On Example

Once you are in redesign, it is easy to branch out in all different directions. One of the easiest add-ons is to become a personal shopper. You are already in your client's home, she already trusts you, and she knows what you have done.

You can say, "You love what I have done for you and know that I have a good eye. I would love to shop for the items that are missing from this room. I charge $X to shop for you and get everything you need ready to go."

Once she agrees, it is time to settle on a budget. You have to have a budget discussion even though no one wants to talk about money. However, going shopping without a budget is like saying to someone, "Go buy me a car." Does the person want a BMW or a Volkswagen? You will not know until you ask.

There is an easy way to have this conversation:

"We have now determined that you need some lamps, some artwork, and a few different basic accessories to fill out your room. If you went into a store today, how much do you think you would want to pay for a lamp?"

The customer says $50.

"What about a little accessory?"

The customer says $20.

"What about a piece of artwork?"

The customer says $3,000.

What you have just found is that the customer does not really care about lamps or accessories, but when it comes to artwork, it had better be good. It also says that you will be shopping at a different store for the artwork.

The beauty of this process is that the client now has given you a budget.

Expert Example

Everyone has his or her own likes and dislikes, and this drives what a person is willing to pay for that item. For example, I do not care about accessories. Paying $17 at Target for a little something is just fine for me.

On the other hand, I love area rugs. I have paid thousands and thousands of dollars for them. A good designer will get to the heart of these likes and dislikes and not assume what a person is willing to pay for an item.

Once a client has given you his prices, this is the time to point out any unrealistic beliefs that the client may have. Buying a lamp for $50 is possible, but finding more than one at that price point might be tough. This is when you explain a realistic price point for the item. The client really might not know and is looking to you for guidance. You can say:

"Let's look at these numbers. You need two lamps, and I can definitely get you two lamps for $100. You need two pieces of artwork, and I can definitely get you some fabulous artwork for $6,000. You wanted to keep all your accessories under $20. We need at least eight things. I definitely can find pieces that fall under $20, but you will end up with eight things under $20, making everything look cheap. I would recommend that we do five accessories under $20 and three accessories under $40. This way you can have a more expensive piece and a less expensive piece together."

At this point, be sure to clarify your fee and if it needs to be incorporated in the numbers you just went through or if it is on top of those numbers. You might say, "For $250, I will shop different stores with a budget of $6,320 and buy your two lamps, two pieces of artwork, and eight accessories. I cannot wait to find the perfect items for your home."

There is no doubt that your client will be happy once he has seen his new awesome, finished room or has had you do additional services for him. Now you need to learn how to keep the client happy.

Happy Clients Grow Your Business

Think of the last time you had service work done for you — either for your home or your business. Let us say you worked with a business coach for six weeks to develop a project. The job is now over, and it is four weeks later. Did you hear from the business coach? Did you get an e-mail saying she hoped your project was going well? Did you find out about other services she offers that might help you?

If the answer is yes, your business coach was using the easiest marketing tool available to a business — keeping clients happy. Keeping a current client is much less expensive than finding a new client, yet businesspeople let clients disappear after the project is complete.

Do not let the fear of bothering your client with a sales call stop you from checking in. Calling to see how someone is doing after you have worked with him is simply courteous and shows you care. No one is going to perceive that as bothersome.

Once you have your client vocalize how much she appreciated your service, you can help her again by letting her know of another specific service you provide that also may serve her needs. This will be perceived as helpful since she already knows and trusts you and is delighted with what you offer. This keeps her from having to go find someone else to do the work needed.

Even if your client was not happy with your service, calling is still advantageous. Studies show that, if you make a mistake and correct it, the loyalty to your service is even higher than for those whom you pleased from the onset. Following up is the best thing you can do for client relationships.

Ask the Expert

Q. I completed a redesign with a customer, and she was happy with my service. However, I do not know what kind of follow-up conversations to have. Help!

A. Your job is not done when you think it is done. Just because your client is happy and gave you the check, the worst thing that you can do is pretend that it is over.

You should call back in two days and say something like, "Are you still in shock over your lovely room?" or "What did your husband have to say? Is he just as excited as you?" This gives your client the opportunity to express her gratitude once again.

Ask the Expert

Then, maybe two weeks later, write a little note that says, "I am shopping for a client, and I saw this perfect green vase that would look lovely in your home. I just wanted to let you know that if you are out shopping, Target has it on sale." You are not saying, "Hey, come to me to get it." Instead, you have just added tremendous value to what you do. They do not have to buy the vase. They do not have to pay you again. However, should they want to have you shop for them, they know where you are.

In about six weeks, you write to them and say, "I thought I would drop you a line. I am sure you still love your home. Call me if you ever need another redesign or if you have a friend who can use my services."

As time goes by, the contacts can decrease. However, eventually, you will find that your customer becomes a repeat customer. Remember, it is seven times more expensive to get a new customer than it is to keep an old customer. You keep your clients by showing that you care.

• ◆ ⌘ ◆ •

Mary's Trade Tips

Always return your phone calls. You have something to gain by returning calls — a client. This may sound obvious, but if you are in business and your phone rings, you need to be answering it or at the very least returning calls within 24 hours. It is amazing to me how many people I have talked to who are looking for clients and yet tell me they do not return phone calls promptly. This is a surefire way to not get a client.

For a quick checklist of the redesign process see Appendix 1.

The next chapter helps you move beyond the beginning stages of your business. Read it now and mark it for later. These "extra" ideas will help you as your business grows.

Chapter 10

As Your Business Grows

*W*hat you know and do when you first start your business is far different from what you will know and do a year later. You should understand that the business of redesign, redecorating, and real estate staging is ongoing. You should not stop growing and learning.

Wider World Wide Web

Blog

A blog is a type of Web site that is arranged in chronological order from the most recent entry, known as a post, at the top of the main page to the older entries toward the bottom. Blogs are written by one person and are updated regularly. For the purpose of your business, your blog should be on the topic of redesign, redecorating, and real estate staging.

Business blogs can be a good choice for both large and small companies. Most large companies already have a profile on the Internet, but smaller companies struggle to get visitors and have serious problems reaching people interested in their field of business. A good way to change this is to start a blog.

Here are reasons you may wish to start a blog:

- **You know your field of business the best.** If you are running your own business, you obviously know what you are doing. If you create a blog, this will further your expertise in the field. Sharing your knowledge will help others see you as a professional.

- **Reach more people.** Your site may include various sections, but people may not be able to access this information unless they are existing customers. Creating a blog will help you find new readers and customers.

- **Coverage.** Your blog can be used as a method of communication with existing customers, as well as the whole world. You can use the blog to provide information about new products and create excitement.

- **Will the idea work?** If you have plans to expand your product line or even go in a different direction, you can include these thoughts in your blog. Readers will be more than happy to offer their opinions. This way you can find out if your plans will make your customers happy.

- **Customer relationship.** When you acquire a new customer, you want to do everything in your power to keep that customer. A blog is a good way to interact with existing and new customers.

- **Host your blog on your main Web site.** More readers means more links to your blog. In turn, this translates to better search engine placement, effectively advertising your blog and your Web site.

For some great blog examples visit:

- **www.YourDesignBizBlog.com** — even more design biz tips

- **www.BuildaBetterBlog.com** — all things blog related

Automated E-mail Campaigns

Keeping your clients happy is essential. One good way to do this is through an automated e-mail campaign. An automated e-mail campaign consists of scheduled, prewritten e-mails to your clients. Such e-mails can include newsletters, tips, announcements, holiday greetings, and reminders. Customers of a business are happy to hear about further information once the initial relationship has begun.

To be successful in e-mail marketing, the idea is to broadcast your message to as many people as you possibly can. At the same time, the need to maintain the respect and privacy of your existing and potential customers needs to be taken into account.

The primary rule of e-mail marketing is that it is permission-based. Without permission, sending advertising to a potential customer is not only rude but also illegal, and heavy fines can be imposed on your company. The place to start with e-mail marketing campaigns is with existing customers of your business.

The graphical style of the e-mail newsletter should complement your Web site. The content contained in it needs to get to the point quickly. There needs to be a call to action so that your readers will be inclined to contact you.

As your business grows, you may find it harder to keep up with all your e-mail contacts and the e-mails you wish to send. In this case, you may want to consider using an e-mail campaign service. Such services include Constant Contact, SaleAmp, and MailChimp.

Craigslist.org

Craiglist, an online community, features classified ads for such things as jobs, housing, personals, for sale/wanted, services, and community events, all for free. These ads are grouped into like categories.

This Web site boasts a top-ten ranking in terms of page views. More than ten million people visit the site each month. Craiglist is featured in 175 cities and 34 countries.

••⌘••

Mary's Trade Tips

Craigslist will not work for all redesigners and stagers. It depends on your niche. If you work with stay-at-home moms, you may be successful using Craigslist because these potential clients are a large part of the network base. Businesswomen, on the other hand, are a much smaller portion of Craigslist users. If you are targeting the For Sale By Owner client as a stager, consider posting your ads in the real estate services section.

Link Exchanges

Link exchange, also referred to as reciprocal link exchange, involves exchanging links with other industry-related Web sites. You can establish a reciprocal link by e-mailing another Web site owner and asking him or her to link to your site if you link to his or hers.

••⌘••
_____

Mary's Trade Tips

If you always use a certain paint or rug store or always use a specific artist, ask them to do a link exchange with you. This means that their traffic will be able to click to your site, and your traffic can click to theirs. It is a free and easy way to increase your visibility to potential clients.

_____

A Lens

Viral marketing is about getting people to visit your site, buy your product, or get your ideas to spread. This has led to search engine optimization (SEO), Google AdWords, banners, online copywriting, blogs, and tags. The Lens is a new tool for the same purpose.

With a lens, you can create your personal page (a lens) and can add content, such as news, RSS feeds, links, and your own content, like text and images. You also can earn money with your lens. Go to **www.squidoo.com** to start your own lens.

Webinars

A high tech way to give a class is to give a Webinar, which is short for Web-based seminar. A Webinar is any sort of presentation, lecture, workshop, or seminar transmitted over the Web. A key feature of a Webinar is its interactive elements. In a Webinar, the presenter and participants have the ability to give, receive, and discuss information.

The purpose of a Webinar is to:

- Build awareness of your business

- Position your business as a leader

- Generate client leads

Despite the marketing goals of your Webinar, it should not include any marketing or sales content. Doing so will ruin your credibility and turn away potential customers.

A typical format of a good webinar includes:

1. **An introduction.** Introduce yourself and give a brief biography to establish yourself as a credible speaker on the topic of redesign.

2. **A presentation:** Give a 20-minute presentation with seven to ten slides. As a rule, you should have one slide for every two to three minutes of talking. You also will want to show an outline of what will be discussed and, throughout the presentation, show people where you are with respect to the outline.

3. **A Q&A session.** Allow for a 10- to 15-minute Q&A discussion of questions from attendees.

To prevent people from falling asleep or being bored, you should make your presentation as interesting and dynamic as possible. Also be sure that your slides are well designed and your content is appropriate and engaging.

For a Webinar to be successful, you will need to promote it:

- You should promote your Webinar with some sort of advertising campaign at least two or three weeks before its scheduled date.

- You should advertise your Webinar on your Web site, preferably in a place where many people will see it.

- Consider customizing the signature line of your e-mail so that it includes the date of the Webinar and a link to the registration page on your Web site.

- Write a press release about the Webinar and include details about why it is valuable to your clients and how to register.

- Send out an e-mail to all your clients, telling them about your Webinar.

- Four to five days before the event, send out a reminder e-mail to all those who have registered for your Webinar.

After you have completed the Webinar, you can use the information again in your marketing and PR campaigns. Since you dedicated a lot of time to your Webinar, it makes sense to get as much use out of the information as possible.

Here are some tips:

- Archive each Webinar you host and post it on your Web site. In addition to this, be sure to post a description of each Webinar.

- Submit the URL of the page on which all your Webinars are listed to major search engines.

- When your Webinar is over, write another press release that summarizes the event and includes some of the most pertinent question and answer topics you discussed.

Although you can host your own Webinar, it would take a lot of time and technology experience. Outsourcing is a better option because other companies can handle logistics, hosting, archiving, and results tracking. Here are a few good companies that offer Webinar hosting:

- On24 (**http://on24.com**)

- WebEx (**http://webex.com**)

- Intercall (**http://www.intercall.com/home.htm**)

- Bulldog Solutions (**http://www.bulldogsolutions.com/ leadgeneration.php**)

- Talking Communities (**http://talkingcommunities.com**)

More Marketing Methods

It Is Time to Say It

Radio and television advertisements stick in people's minds much more than print advertising. This is because people remember sound more easily than print. Most of us do not remember the state capitals we learned in elementary school, but if we hear a song from our youth, the words all come rushing back.

In addition to being memorable, audio allows you to show off your personality. Instead of your Web site stating what you do and how you do it, an audio clip can make your Web site feel more like a personal interview.

There are many different ways to use audio clips on your Web site. Here are just a few:

1. A description of each of your services

2. Why you feel that redesign, redecorating, or real estate staging is so wonderful

3. Your policies and pricing

4. A personal invitation to call you

5. Your latest radio interview

6. Your presentation schedule

The possibilities are endless.

More important than what you say, however, is how you say it. Be enthusiastic about your services.

By the time you consider adding audio to your Web site, you already will have established a good working relationship with a Web designer. If you have not, it is time to do so.

T-shirts, Key Chains, and More

Promotional products offer a unique opportunity to get your company's name out to its target market and keep it there.

•◆⌘◆•

Mary's Trade Tips

Place a gift bag with a related inexpensive gift in it on the door of every new listing in your market.

The promotional items you choose are limited only by your own creativity. They can range from market-proven goods — such as calendars, coffee mugs, and baseball caps — to innovative items like candy and nuts, stadium blankets, toy cars and trucks, and first-aid kits. Whatever items you pick, all should bear your logo and contact information.

•◆⌘◆•

Mary's Trade Tips

Wearing your business name is a great way to get attention. Giving your name for others to wear is even better. People love T-shirts, so give them what they love. Give them to your client's children or to those who have taken a class. Wear one yourself when you are out in the community. You will be amazed at the conversations it will start.

Rolling Along

If you had a storefront, you certainly would have a sign saying who you are and what you do. Just because you do not have a storefront, however, does not mean that your mobile office should be without signs.

Your car will be visible while you are working. It will be seen all day long as you are driving around town. You might as well use it as a sales tool.

There are several varieties of signs:

- Sign painted onto the car
- Window signs
- Vinyl lettering
- Magnetic signs

No matter which type of sign you choose, be sure that your contact information, including your URL, is clearly visible.

Picture-Perfect Brochures

In the beginning, brochures are not necessary. As you grow, however, you may want to invest in a small number for specific functions. For instance, if you charge money for a class, having a stylish brochure may be appropriate. If you are meeting with a local real estate agents' group, having a full-color brochure may help them remember you and what you do.

To create a good brochure, you need to consider what your target readers will want to know. In redesign, redecorating, and real estate staging, such questions might be:

- What is redesign?

- What services are included?

- Is there a Web site where I can learn more?

- Can I see some "before and after" photos?

Next, you need to entice your reader to turn the page and keep reading. This means that you should not put everything on the front page. Spread out the information to get your reader to look at each page. A good way to do this is to provide several sets of "before and after" photos, placing at least one set per page.

Writing the content for a brochure is far different from writing for an article. Your potential client will not read several paragraphs of information. Instead, brochure content should be written using brief, concise statements. The rule of thumb is that the reader should be able to get the message of the statement in a two-second glance.

Use your business's selling points as headlines. This will encourage your reader to want to know more and to read the supporting details you have provided.

Finally, you want to keep the brochure in his hands and not in the trashcan. You can do this by supplying helpful tips or information that people can reference even if they do not purchase your service. As a redesigner, you might want to explain how to measure windows or give a tip on hanging pictures on the wall.

A Local Picasso

Hanging local art in a home is a great way to give yourself a competitive edge as a real estate stager. Original art, selected to fit the home, can bring color to an otherwise neutral room or create height. It can attract the eye to a beautiful feature of a home. It can give the home warmth.

Artists are eager to put their art into homes for sale because it gets them noticed. They also may be able to sell the art when the house sells. Such art can include paintings, sculpture, and even rugs.

If you work with a particular builder or realtor on a regular basis, he or she may be willing to advertise a grand open house with wine and food that mentions both you and the local artist.

You can use this method in a similar fashion as a redesigner. Have an agreement with a local artist to use her art whenever possible as you redesign a home. When you get to a wall that simply needs a wall hanging that cannot be found in the home, hang work from the local artist. This will help your client's room feel more complete. As with any of the items you place in the home, he can either give it back and purchase something on his own or choose to purchase what you have hanging.

Networking With Online Forums

Forums are online communities in which people can discuss topics of interest to them. People discuss these topics by posting comments to the forum. A discussion is called a "thread," and forums often have several threads going at any time.

Online forums can be a great way to connect with other professionals in your field. If you find someone with a similar business with whom you get along, you might be able to join your businesses together and create a partnership. You may not be so lucky, but you may be able to get referrals and find helpful information.

Forums allow signatures; this means at the end of your post and after your name you can have a descriptive line about your company and then a link to your Web site. This is your advertisement so you want to choose your descriptive line carefully.

Creating the Perfect Tagline

A marketing tagline is the one- or two-line descriptor that comes after a product logo or company name. With some creativity and persistence, you can develop your own tagline.

First, decide what you want to communicate with your tagline. Ask yourself these questions:

1) Who are your customers?

2) What benefits do you give your customers?

3) What feelings do you want to evoke in your customers?

4) What action are you trying to generate from your customers?

5) How are you different from your competition?

Try to get one or more of these across in your tag.

Second, prepare to brainstorm tagline options.

Gather taglines from other companies and brands. Look in other categories besides your own and try to find taglines from both large and small companies.

As you find taglines, write them on index cards or individual slips of paper. You will be mixing and matching them and pairing them with unrelated items as you brainstorm. Pay attention to the words used, how they are put together, and which of the five questions they address. By doing this, you more likely will come up with a unique angle for your own tagline.

To find taglines, look around. You may find them anywhere there are advertisements, packaging, or logos. Look in cupboards, around desks, in magazines, on TV/radio commercials, in print advertisements, and on Web sites.

Find your competitors' taglines — look at them and strive to be better and different.

Gather together books to help you come up with different ways to phrase similar ideas.

Third, brainstorm.

Go through your props. Look up words or concepts in the books. Rearrange your various props so you can look at them in different ways. Write down everything that comes to mind and all the new ideas each phrase sparks. They do not have to make sense. You want a large number of ideas.

Fourth, consolidate your list.

After brainstorming, go through all your ideas. Pull out those few you think have the best potential. Try to reduce longer ones to fewer words.

Fifth, choose the one best tagline.

You should be left with a short list of possibilities. To pick the single best tagline, get others' opinions.

Reprinted With Permission From Erin Ferree, Elf Design

Elfdesign.com

Logo Lingo

As time goes on, you will want to have a logo. The key characteristics of a good logo include:

Consistency in use of your logo, tagline, and materials. Repetition of similar elements, used in the same or similar ways, helps people remember who you are and what you do.

Memorability. This ensures that your logo stays at the forefront in the mind of your potential clients and that they will think of you the next time they have a need.

Uniqueness. This helps you distinguish your company or industry from its competitors. For example, if everyone in your industry uses a particular symbol, try to use something else — this will make your logo look different and uncommon. The uniqueness of a logo guarantees a brand's recognition. Thus, it is important for a logo to be distinctive and, at the same time, appealing.

Professionalism. This can be portrayed in the choice of quality of the graphics, the printing, and the paper on which your materials are printed.

Timelessness. This will ensure that you do not have to redesign your logo in just a few years and that your investment and equity used in your logo design will be lasting.

Differentiation between the colors in your logo. This is just not in terms of hue but in terms of value as well so that it translates well either to black-and-white or grayscale.

Unity among the different elements in the logo. The logo must fit together as a single unit and not just appear as a jumble of elements pasted together.

Scalability. This ensures that your logo looks equally good in every size, be it on a business card, on a sign for your business, or at any size in between. To make your business's name legible at different logo sizes, make sure that your designer chooses a font that is read easily.

Reprinted With Permission From Bobette Kyle

Websitemarketingplan.com

If You Know It, Write It

If you know your subject area and can communicate your ideas in a clear, compelling, organized manner, writing a book is feasible. The reasons for writing a book are:

1) **Create an image for yourself as an "expert" in your field.** When someone has written a book on a topic, he is considered an expert.

2) **It is free publicity.** Writing a book is free advertising for your business.

3) **You could become a top authority.** As you write your book, you will do more research on the subject. If it is really a subject you love and that you already are an expert in, you could become a top authority, as you are inspired to do more research and really understand the topic better.

Here are three good ways to write a book:

25X4X2 System: Take your topic of expertise. Ask yourself, "What are the 25 important main topics regarding this subject matter?" Then come up with about four subtopics for each of these main 25 topics. Write two pages per night on each of these subtopics.

You will end up with a 200-page book in just more than three months.

The One-Page-per-Topic System: Write down all your marketing ideas and then write something on each topic.

••✦⌘✦••
_____

Mary's Trade Tips

I know someone who used this system to put together a book on marketing. He had many ideas that he wanted to share with people so he brainstormed ideas and wrote down every single marketing idea that came to mind. He then wrote something on each topic. Some topics had short "blurbs" and others had five or six pages. After writing, he put the topics into categories that made sense. At the end of this exercise, he had a 265-page book filled with great marketing ideas.

_____

Transcribe-the-Seminar System: This method is particularly effective for those who have difficulty writing. If you do not particularly like writing, you may prefer speaking instead. That being the case, get six or eight of your favorite friends together, sit them down in a nice room, serve cocktails, and deliver a seminar. Make sure you have outlined your topic thoroughly and have divided your presentation into bite-size "modules." These will end up being your chapters when all is said and done.

A big problem people have is editing. This is simply a psychological block, especially if you feel you have to make everything perfect. This is an impossible task. Just get your thoughts down on paper and hire an editor to clean up the first draft.

The cost-effective way to get the book printed is to provide the printer with a camera-ready copy of your manuscript. (Talk to your printer to find out what it needs.) This is referred to as typesetting or layout. You also can provide your manuscript to the printer on a disk, typed in a common word processing program, like Microsoft Word or Corel WordPerfect. There is a fee for taking your manuscript off a disk and preparing it for production.

Shop around. Get quotes from at least three different printers. Check out their previous work. Just because they are cheaper does not mean you are going to get a quality product. When you find a printer, be sure to get a contract. This will help ensure that your expectations, such as price, delivery, and specifications, are met.

Publishing starts with the appearance of the cover. Model your publication after it. Check with the printer you decide to use. It can help you in this area.

So, how many copies should you print? You have three main options:

- Print 2,000 — 5,000 books at a reasonable unit price.

- Print 500 — 1,000 books at a higher unit price.

- Print covers ahead of time and copy your text on demand. This will provide you with a competitive unit price with low, upfront costs.

What factors will affect the cost?

- Book dimensions (6" x 9", 8.5" x 11", and so forth)

- Type of binding (perfect binding, hard bound, comb-bound, saddle stitched, velo-bound, wire-bound)

- Kind of paper used for the cover

- Number of ink colors on cover and in text

- Number of pages in text (count title page, table of contents, index, every page)

- Quantity of books desired

- How prepared your manuscript is

Once you write and register the manuscript, you will own the copyright to the material. It is a matter of filling out a form and sending the required fee to the U.S. Copyright Office at **http:// lcweb.loc.gov/copyright/**.

International Standard Book Numbers (ISBNs) are a unique number assigned to books and publishers, which are assigned and maintained by the ISBN Agency. This number is useful for consumers when trying to locate books. It is also necessary if you want to sell your books in bookstores. For more information about ISBNs contact the U.S. ISBN Agency at **http://www.isbn .org/standards/home/isbn/us/index.asp**.

You can find a ghostwriter by conducting an online search for "ghostwriter" or checking **www.elance.com**. To learn more about hiring a writer, check out **www.hiringawriter.blogspot.com**.

Upgrade the Web Site

"Call Me Now" Button

With a "Call Me Now" button, an interested prospect who is on your Web site can click a button and reach you on the phone. All your Web visitor has to do is enter her name, phone number, and e-mail address, and she is connected to your business, live, via phone.

This is a wonderful way to have potential clients see your Web site and ask questions of you before they leave the page. People visit a Web site to gather information before a purchase. If they are unable to get their questions answered quickly or painlessly, there is a danger of losing that prospect.

As a bonus for you, "Call Me Now" collects the potential client's contact information so you will have her in your system.

Add Sticky Content

Sticky content is information on your Web site that gives users a reason for coming back again and again. The goal is to get someone to share his contact information with you or for him to contact you to get more information.

Some sticky content to include on your Web site might be:

- Interactive floor plans
- Demographics for area home sales
- An interactive color wheel (see **http://kuler.adobe.com/** and **http://www.firemountaingems.com/beading_how tos/beading_projects.asp?docid=6912**)
- Weekly decorating tips
- A blog
- Tip of the day
- RSS news feed on decorating or staging topics
- New "before and after" photo of the week
- A contest
- Color tricks (see **http://www.Sanford-artedventures .com/study/m_a_tricks.html**)

When you figure out what works on your site, it will work repeatedly.

Video Room Tour Stagers and Redesigners

Web-based video tours are a winning marketing strategy for real estate agents. They make a house come alive for a prospective buyer. The video tour allows agents to get a true picture of every square inch of the house and its flow.

Although you do not have a home to sell, you do have your services to sell. Using a video room tour is a great way to show what you have done with a room or an entire home. Photos are great, but a video can convey so much more.

With a video, you can highlight everything from the staged backyard to redesigning techniques that make architectural details pop to special additions you bought or created. A video allows you to lead your potential clients through your redesigned room the way you would a friend.

Here are tips to help you create an effective video:

1. Make a list of everything you like best about the house and pick the top five to highlight.

2. Open the window shades to capture the house in the best possible light. The best way to avoid a dark video is to buy a video camera that excels in low light. You can read many reviews online of camcorders, and they all address this issue. Some definitely do better in low light than others do. Secondly, turning on all the lights in the house helps tremendously. Hauling around big lights is not necessary if you have the right camera and light the house properly.

3. Remember to show every room and any special features that can be overlooked in a photo.

4. Add a brief narration to guide your potential clients

during your walkthrough. You even can say things to help your potential client imagine herself using your great service. Your narration needs to tell a story, whether it is an audio narration or title slides. There is no need to insult your Web guest by stating the obvious. Instead, be expressive and paint a word story using emotion and excitement. People redesign their homes based on emotion.

5. Buy a tripod to get rid of shakiness. This is a good idea even if you are taking still photos. You will want a solid tripod with a fluid head to keep your pans steady. If you want to do video by panning around a room, all you need is a tripod and a good camera. If you want to do a walkthrough, walking from room to room or down hallways, which definitely gives a better feel for the room and the layout and relationship between rooms, you will need a steadicam.

6. Find simple video editing software to help you present the best view of the house to your potential clients. Regardless of whether you use your video on a Web site, on a CD/DVD, or on a video podcast, you will need to edit your video. On Windows, there is Windows Movie Maker program. On the Mac, there is iMovie.

7. A good microphone is essential. Do not bother with your built-in mic. If you are going to all the trouble to make a great video, you do not want the audio to make your video look amateurish.

8. A music background is essential to create the "mood," but it also can be distracting if you choose the incorrect music. Be sure that you have checked licenses and royalty issues on any music you choose to use. The easiest way to

avoid legal issues is to use royalty-free music. Just search Google for "royalty free music" or "podcast music," and you can find all sorts of great background music free of any licensing fees. Choose your music carefully — not everyone has your taste. The goal is to sell your service, so do not have your music compete for the attention of the viewer. You want viewers to focus on the property, not the music.

If you are willing to buy the proper equipment (camera, tripod, steadicam, and computer software) and practice, practice, practice, the results will be incredible and will show your potential clients what you can do for them.

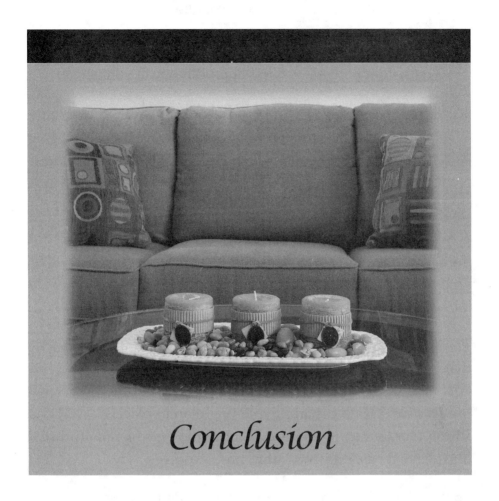

Conclusion

*W*e live in an age of increasing specialization. You see this specialization in technology, where one company does only Web site design and another does only Web site hosting. You also see it in health care, where a doctor performs only facial plastic surgery or a dentist works only with children. This specialization holds true in interior design as well and has given rise to the concepts of redesign, redecorating, and real estate staging.

Now that you have read this book, the resources to start your own redesign or real estate staging business are at your fingertips. There is no one right way to run your business. How you use these ideas is up to you.

Important concepts learned are:

1) Customize these business approaches to fit your situation.

2) Conditions are different in every market.

3) Success in the redesign, redecorating, and real estate staging business is a matter of both design and business practices.

The creative portion of the business requires that you create a room or home that fits the needs of your client, whether that need is to beautify for personal use or appeal to a broad audience for the sale of the home. Your sense of balance and color, as well as your attention to detail, will make your business stand out from the competition.

The business practices you use also will set you apart. It is true that anyone can open a business by simply getting a license and obtaining clients. However, as this book has outlined, you will need a sound business and marketing plan in place, as well as a strong work ethic, to succeed. Those who persevere and thrive must have focus, diligence, time, and resources.

Look to the different chapters in this book. Peruse the appendices. Try the different marketing methods. Talk to your colleagues. Talk to your clients. Most importantly, take the plunge into the fabulous world of redesign, redecorating, and real estate staging.

Good luck with all your business endeavors!

Appendix

Appendix 1: Redesign Steps

- Talk to the client — determine the needs of the client and the purpose of the room.

- Take "before" pictures.

- Break down the room and create a holding area.

- Determine the focal point of the room.

- Evaluate the shape of the room.

- Place the largest piece of upholstery first.

- Shop the home for items from other rooms.

- Place the area rug.

- Finish placing the furniture, working down in size.

- Place lighting.

- Place tall plants or trees.

- Place artwork.

- Begin to accessorize on focal wall.

- Take "after" photos.

- Create shopping list.

Appendix 2: Real Estate Staging Evaluation Form

Real Estate Staging Evaluation Form

MARY LARSEN
DESIGNS

EVERY HOME HAS A STORY TO TELL

Your home is quite possibly the biggest asset that you possess. Now that your home is for sale, it is no longer your home, but rather a house — a product for sale — and you want to achieve its maximum dollar value.

The following evaluation is designed to give your house a competitive edge in today's market and is the first line of defense over the need to lower your price.

Be sure to keep in mind that the way we live in our homes is very different from the way we sell our homes.

Real Estate Staging Evaluation Form

By implementing the following suggestions, you will increase your chances of getting top dollar for your home in the minimum amount of time needed.

Name: _____ Date: _____

Address: _____

City: _____ State: _____ Zip: _____

Agent: _____

Company: _____

Address: _____

City: _____ State: _____ Zip: _____

Phone: _____ Cell: _____

E-mail Address: _____

Objective

Your objective is for every potential buyer to feel as though your house is his home. We want to highlight the unique characteristics of your home and give the buyer a "reason" to buy. We want him to "feel" that the space is his own so he can picture himself living there.

Buyers have a hard time imagining how a room could be used, so we have to show them. Buyers only know what they see, not the way it is going to be.

For Every Home

- Remove all personal items, such as family photos and personal collections.

- Clean every room and surface, including baseboards, cabinetry, windows, and light fixtures.

- Declutter everywhere.

- Deodorize every room.

- Be sure all pet items (food dishes and litter boxes) are in an out-of-sight location, such as the garage or laundry room.

Real Estate Staging Evaluation Form

- Reduce clutter in closets so that only half the closet is full.

- Arrange all kitchen cabinets so that they resemble a store shelf.

- Remove any excess furniture or stored items to a storage facility.

- Consider painting your interior a neutral color.

Exterior Home Staging Review

House Exterior: _____
Landscaping: _____
Driveway, Walks, Steps: _____
Decks, Porches, Patios: _____
Deck: _____
Garage, Carport: _____
Roof: _____
Yard: _____

Interior Home Staging Review

For every room, evaluate the following:

- Walls, wallpaper, paint
- Cabinet contents

- Floors
- Counter clutter

- Wall art, photos
- Window treatments, windows

- Accessories
- Light fixtures

- Scatter rugs
- Caulk and grout

- Junk drawer
- Cabinet and appliance surfaces

- Develop a more specific list for each room — for example, the front and top of the fridge in the kitchen, the items hanging on the door in the entryway, and so on.

Living Room: _____
Dining Room: _____
Kitchen: _____

Real Estate Staging Evaluation Form

Family Room: _____

Office: _____

Master Bedroom: _____

Bathrooms: _____

Master Closet: _____

Bedroom #2: _____

Bedroom #3: _____

Hallway: _____

Storage: _____

Laundry Room: _____

Conclusion: _____

Home Staging Review

Priorities:

1. _____

2. _____

3. _____

4. _____

5. _____

Other: _____

_____

_____

Thank you for the pleasure and the opportunity of working with you!

Appendix 3: Contract

Contract

MARY LARSEN DESIGNS

EVERY HOME HAS A STORY TO TELL

3340 Langston Circle
Apex, NC 27539
919-773-1445
mary@marylarsendesigns.com
www.MaryLarsenDesigns.com

Customer Contract

On this the _____ day of _____ year of _____, Mary Larsen
Designs enters into a contract with _____ to do the following
work at this address: _____

_____

_____ .

This work includes the following:

_____

_____

_____

_____

Terms and Conditions:

1. All information must be written and signed. Verbal information given in
person or over the phone is not part of the contract.

2. Merchandise that is made to order may not be returned.

Contract

3. There will be a $35 fee for returned checks.

4. The homeowner is responsible for all color choices. Although Mary Larsen or one of her associates will assist the homeowner in a color choice, final decisions are the responsibility of the homeowner.

5. All dates of product delivery are based on normal delivery times. Product delivery held up by a third party is not the responsibility of Mary Larsen Designs.

6. Any legal fees associated with a dispute of this contract will be paid by the party determined to be in the wrong.

7. Installation is part of the price of this contract unless otherwise stated.

I have read and understand the above conditions for doing business with Mary Larsen Designs.

_____   _____

Homeowner and Date   Mary Larsen, Mary Larsen Designs

Appendix 4: Tools of the Trade

It is imperative that you are prepared for your room redesign — and the tools that you have with you will make all the difference in the world. These are the tools you cannot live without:

- Mark-it level
- Scissors
- Wire cutter
- Screwdriver
- Museum or poster putty
- Rubber bands

- Step stool
- Sharpie marker
- Straight and safety pins
- Flashlight
- Pencil and chalk
- Painter's tape
- Floral sheers and tape
- Masking and Scotch tape
- Hammer, nails, picture hanging wire, wall anchors, and picture hanging kit
- Rechargeable cordless drill and batteries
- Furniture touch-up sticks or pens
- Lint brush and wrinkle-release spray
- Furniture movers for both carpet and hardwoods
- Other items for decorating: greenery, floral foam, plate stands, old books, fabric scraps, small accessories, curtain rods and rings, sheer drapes

Appendix 5: Class Topic Suggestions

- Does Your Room Need a Doctor?
- Diagnosing Your Room's Ailments
- Addicted to Decorating
- Spring Decorating
- The Power of Placement
- Tips for a Beautiful Room
- The Art of Accessorizing
- Picture-Perfect Picture Placement
- Bring the Outside In

- The Seven Deadly Sins of Decorating
- One-Day Decorating for Busy Moms

Appendix 6: Presentation Folder List

- Two-pocket folder with logo and contact information on a sticker
- At least two business cards
- Two or more postcards
- Evaluation form
- Collage of photos showing your work
- Other information about your business, tips sheet, newsletter, and so forth

Appendix 7: Presentation Guest Evaluation Form

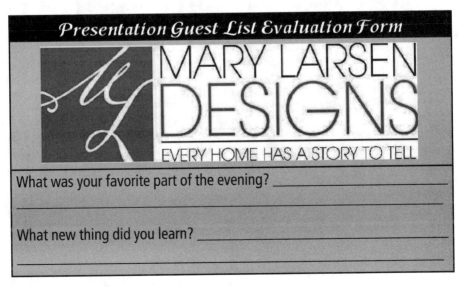

Presentation Guest List Evaluation Form

What would you like to learn more about? _____

_____

If you could add or take something out of the program, what would you
do? _____

_____

Any additional comments? _____

_____

_____

Appendix 8: Prize Giveaway Entry Form

Prize Giveaway entry Form

MARY LARSEN
DESIGNS
EVERY HOME HAS A STORY TO TELL

Name: _____

Address: _____

Phone: _____

E-mail: _____

Would you be interested in receiving a newsletter by e-mail or mail? _____

Would you like me to call you to set up a consultation? _____

Appendix 9: Letter to Introduce Your Business

January 1, XXXX

Dear Friends,

I am excited to announce that, effective January 3, XXXX, I will be providing custom interior design services for the home. My company, Mary Larsen Designs, will provide design consultation and creation services. This includes everything from in-home consultations on window treatment and color suggestions, room arrangement, and accessory suggestions to the actual design, construction, and installation of window treatments, bedding, and baby room designs, such as bed skirts, coverlets, pillows, and shams.

I have been sewing and designing for more than 20 years, and my background includes a bachelor's degree in clothing and textiles from Virginia Tech, as well as several years of design work in the industry. Among them, I was an assistant designer for Christian Dior wedding gowns, and the tips and techniques I acquired transfer nicely into home design work. This experience also greatly influences the design and construction process of my distinctive christening gowns, which I also will be offering.

My research into this business venture has shown that the only way to get started and to be successful is by word-of-mouth referrals. That is why you are receiving this letter — you are my network. If you or any of your friends are considering custom work for your home — perhaps even looking for furniture or wood blinds — give me a call. And yes, for those of you wondering, I will continue my current employment as well.

I have enclosed a couple of my business cards. One is for your files; the other is for anyone you know who may have a need for my services. I would appreciate any referrals you are able to provide.

If you have any questions about my services, please feel free to contact me by phone or e-mail — 123-456-7890 or mary@ marylarsendesigns.com.

Thank you for your help and friendship.

With warm regards for a prosperous New Year,

Mary Larsen

Appendix 10: Welcome to the Neighborhood Letter

September 5, XXXX

Welcome to the Neighborhood!

I hope your move has gone smoothly, and you are enjoying your new surroundings.

Mary Larsen Designs is a full-service interior design firm based right next door in Langston. We specialize in window treatments and anything to do with fabric. Our goal is to help personalize your home through interior design with you in mind. We help create an environment that genuinely belongs to you, combining new elements, such as color, texture, and accessories, with your existing treasured pieces. We strongly believe that good design should be filled with character and personality, and your interior and its pieces should tell your unique story.

Call us at 123-456-7890 to discover the untold story in your home.

Again — congratulations and welcome!

Appendix 11: Customer To-Do Checklist

Things to Do for Customer Files

- Customer contact sheet
- Measurements
- Digital pictures
- Sort and rename miscellaneous pictures

Initial Visit Checklist

- Portfolio of my work
- Ideas from other sources
- Magazine/sourcing books
- Pencil
- Calculator
- Sample books
- Anything determined in initial phone call
- Step ladder
- Measuring tape
- Notebook
- Pen
- Digital camera

Every Visit

- Step ladder
- Notebook
- Pen
- Measuring tape
- Pencil
- Calculator

- Digital camera
- Sample books
- Anything determined previously

Customer File

- Design
- Estimates
- Time spent
- Include estimate of how long I thought it would take
- Install and completion dates

Stats to Consider

- Visit date
- Written estimate date
- Date I got permission
- If COM, date I got fabric
- Date I completed
- Date I let customer know
- Date we set to install
- Date I billed
- Date I collected
- Follow-up date
- What did I send?
- Did I get a response?
- In what way did I follow up?

Appendix 12: Client Contact Form

Client Contact Form

Name:_____

Spouse and/or children's names and ages: _____
_____
_____

Address:_____
_____

How did you hear of us?_____

Home Number:_____

Office Number:_____

Fax Number:_____

Cell Number:_____

E-mail:_____

Why are you calling today? _____
_____
_____

How do you prefer to be contacted? _____

Notes: _____
_____
_____

Appendix 13: Pre-Appointment Question Form

Pre Appointment Question Form

Can you tell me a bit about what you are looking for? _____
_____
_____

Did you just move into town? If so, from where? _____
_____

Have you ever had redesign/redecorating/real estate staging work done before? _____

What kind of concerns do you have? _____
_____
_____

What are you thinking of investing? _____

When do you anticipate making your decision? _____

When would be a good time for you and your spouse to meet with me? ____
_____

Appendix 14: Appointment Confirmation Letter

Appointment Confirmation Letter

MARY LARSEN DESIGNS

EVERY HOME HAS A STORY TO TELL

3340 Langston Circle
Apex, NC 27539
919-773-1445
mary@marylarsendesigns.com
www.MaryLarsenDesigns.com

Dear _____,

It was a pleasure speaking with you about your home. and I am so looking forward to our appointment where we can get to know each other even better. Per our discussion, here are the details of our appointment:

You appointment is _____ at _____.

You have scheduled a:

Redesign_____

Consultation_____

Other_____

My fees, due at the conclusion of our meeting, are as follows:

_____

_____

Thank you again, and I look forward to meeting with you.

Mary Larsen

Appendix 15: Invoice

MARY LARSEN
DESIGNS
EVERY HOME HAS A STORY TO TELL

Invoice

Date	Invoice #
4/1/2007	338

Mary Larsen Designs
3340 Langston Circle
Apex, NC 27539
(919) 773-1445
www.marylarsendesigns.com

Teri B Clark
Maple Street
Small Town, NC 12345

Due Date	Project
4/13/2007	Living Room ...

Item	Description	Amount
consult	Consultation - In clients home to discuss color and fabric selection	0.00

Sales Tax (6.75%)	$0.00
Total	$0.00
Payments	$0.00
Balance Due	$0.00

Mary Larsen Designs - 3340 Langston Circle - Apex - NC 27539 - (919) 773-1445
www.GrowYourDesignBiz.com - Mary@MaryLarsenDesigns.com - www.MaryLarsenDesigns.com

Appendix 16: Client Statistics Form

- What time did the call come in?

- Was a message left?

- How quickly did I return the call?

- If I left a message, when?

- How quickly was the call returned to me?

- Who referred the customer?

- Was a thank-you sent?

- How did the customer hear of me?

- Visit date

- Written estimate date

- Date I got permission

- Estimated time for project

- Date I completed

- Date I billed

- Date I collected

- Actual time spent on project

- Follow-up date

- In what way did I follow up?

- What did I send?

- Did I get a response?

Appendix 17: Weekly Phone Statistics Form

Week of_____

- How many calls came in each day?

Monday_____

Tuesday_____

Wednesday_____

Thursday_____

Friday_____

Saturday_____

Sunday_____

- Who called? At what time? Were they looking for a price, a meeting, or a purchase? Did it turn into an appointment?

1._____

_____

_____

2._____

_____

_____

3._____

_____

_____

4._____

_____

_____

5._____

_____

_____

What have I sold? When? _____

_____

What is the busiest day?

- For office work?_____

- For visits?_____

- For sales?_____

Appendix 18: Revenue and Expense Report Template

Revenue Expense Report Template					
Expense:	Week of:				
Day	From Where?	Item	Amount	For What?	For Whom?

Appendix 19: Online Article Submission Sites

Writing articles is a good way to establish yourself as a professional. In addition to submitting articles to your local newspapers and magazines, you also can submit articles online.

Be sure that you include an author biography at the end of each article. This bio should include who you are, what you do, and a way to contact you. Do not forget to use your Web site URL.

Here are a few article sites you can check out:

- **www.goarticles.com**

- **www.articledashboard.com**

- **www.ideamarketers.com**

- **www.reprintarticles.com**

- **www.ezinearticles.com**

- **www.easyarticles.com**

- **www.articleblast.com**

Appendix 20: Free Software and Computer Classes

OpenOffice.org

Buying Microsoft Office can be a large expense as you first get started in your business. There is an alternative suite of office products, called OpenOffice, that is free.

Like Microsoft Office, OpenOffice has word processing, spreadsheet, presentation, and drawing programs. You can open and save files in a variety of formats, including Microsoft Office, PDF, HTML, and others.

OpenOffice.org is very similar to Microsoft Office, so you will not have to spend a great deal of time growing accustomed to the program.

www.openoffice.org

AirSet

Juggling your time as you start your business and as it grows may be a daunting task. At AirSet, you can create calendars and manage contacts, tasks, and notes. You get one gigabyte of storage for files. You can decide what to share with others.

www.airset.com

YouSendIt

As a redesigner, you may find it necessary to send photos to others by e-mail. Perhaps you are sending some photos to your Web designer or to a local magazine that is printing your article. Perhaps a potential client would like to see some photos before the first consultation. The problem is that photos are often too large to send via e-mail and Internet service providers may reject them.

With YouSendIt, you can send files up to 100 megabytes in size. You type in the recipient's e-mail, and he or she will receive a message that includes a link where they can download your file. For those who send large files on a regular basis, you can sign up for the site's paid service.

www.yousendit.com

Office Accounting Express 2007

Microsoft's Office Accounting Express 2007 is designed for small businesses. Its features can help you with invoicing, payroll, profit and loss reporting, and more. In addition, this program provides you with access to eBay, PayPal, and credit card processing services.

Office Accounting Express 2007 is compatible with other Office programs. The program allows you to customize forms using Word, to sync with contact information in Outlook, and to use information from QuickBooks, Money, Excel, or Access.

www.ideawins.com

Free Online Computer Classes

If you are new to computers, you may want to take classes to help you understand the Internet and use the Microsoft Office or Open Office products. The GFC Global Learning site (**http://www.gcflearnfree.org/**) offers free online classes. You can either take a tutorial and move at your own pace or sign up for an instructor-led class.

Here is a listing of the offered classes:

- Computer Basics
- Windows XP
- Internet Basics
- E-mail Basics
- Office XP
- Word 2002 (XP)
- PowerPoint 2002 (XP)
- Excel 2002 (XP)
- Access 2002 (XP)

Office 2003 has the same series of tutorials as Office XP:

- OpenOffice.org: Writer
- OpenOffice.org: Calc
- Openoffice.Org: Impress

Appendix 21: Business Books Recommended by Mary Larsen

1. Jack Canfield — *The Success Principles: How to Get From Where You Are to Where You Want to Be*

   A comprehensive view of the things you can do to help you reach your goals. Read it all the way through — and then refer back as needed.

2. Frank Bettger — *How I Raised Myself From Failure to Success in Selling*

   An oldie but a goodie. A great introduction to how paying attention to the "little things" in your business can make a big difference.

3. Harry Beckwith — *Selling the Invisible: A Field Guide to Modern Marketing* and *What Clients Love: A Field Guide to Growing Your Business*

   Anything by Harry Beckwith is worth reading. These two are filled with short examples of business guidelines that will help you develop your business.

4. Alan Weiss — *Getting Started in Consulting, Second Edition*

   The best of the best in regards to consulting. No matter what you are selling, in the end, you are all consultants.

5. Jane Pollack — *Soul Proprietor: 101 Lessons From a Life Style Entrepreneur*

   Great business stories that can help you along your own business path.

6. Gail Evans — *Play Like A Man, Win Like A Woman*

For all the women out there — a great way to gain some insight into men and women in the workplace and the differences in work, thinking, and behavior. Moreover, men, it would be an insightful book for you, too.

7. Stephen R. Covey — *The 7 Habits of Highly Effective People*

A classic look into what it takes to be successful.

8. Malcolm Gladwell — *The Tipping Point: How Little Things Can Make a Big Difference*

A fascinating book regarding why some things make it big and others do not. It will give you a new perspective.

9. Martin E. P. Seligman — *Authentic Happiness*

Excellent book on realizing your potential by doing what you love to do.

10. Napoleon Hill — *Think and Grow Rich*

Intriguing book that explains how "rich thinking" leads to rich lives.

11. Teri B. Clark — *301 Simple Things You Can Do to Sell Your Home NOW and For More Money Than You Thought*

A comprehensive book on the ins and outs of home staging. Mary Trochlil Larsen is a featured designer in the book.

Appendix 22: Color in Decorating

Warm Colors — Think the colors of the sun: red, orange, and yellow. When using a cool color on a wall, the wall will appear to advance, making a room feel smaller and more intimate. Avoid using warm colors in a room that is already warm; viewing a warm color actually can make a room feel warmer.

Cool Colors — Think soothing shades of water: blues, greens, and purples. When using a cool color on a wall, the wall will appear to recede, making a room feel larger and more airy. Cool colors are great in a room that is filled with sunlight, since viewing a cool color actually can make a room feel cooler.

Connecting Colors — Colors from the tan, brown, beige, white, and gray family. These colors work to connect rooms, as well as to create a background for more vibrant color combinations.

Red — Hot and spicy and known to actually raise your heart rate. Red is great in a dining room (count how many restaurants you know that use red in their color theme) because it is thought to increase a person's appetite. It also often is used in bedrooms to add a sensuous touch. Many designers say that a bit of red should be used in every room in the house.

Orange — Orange has been known to actually make people feel nervous and edgy. It is a high-energy color and is great as an unexpected color burst in a room. When you are decorating a room, orange is much more daring than red. It can be used to energize a dull room, such as the laundry room or mud room.

Yellow — Though often thought of as sunshiney and happy, yellow is a very tricky color to use when decorating. It is very easy for yellow to have green undertones, which quickly turns the color to an almost sickly shade. Golden yellows and buttery yellows work best in decorating.

Blue — The color blue is known to physically lower a person's blood pressure and decrease a person's appetite. It is not advisable to use blue in a kitchen, since your decrease in appetite might make you think that the food you cook does not taste good. Blue and white is a classic combination and is re-interpreted in decorating trends every few years, as seen in wedgewood, country, and navy blue.

Green — The saying "green is serene" exists for a reason. As a dominant color in nature, green does double duty in that it is both energizing and relaxing at the same time. This combination makes green a perfect choice for offices. Green is also recommended for bedrooms and living rooms, as green is known as peaceful, rejuvenating, and refreshing.

Brown — In former design periods brown translated to "blah." Today brown is the new black and goes with everything. A rich, deep brown (think chocolate bar) can be used with almost every other color — red, black, hot pink, orange, lime green, powder blue — you name it. Dark brown is versatile and can be worked into almost any color scheme.

Pink — Not just for little girls anymore. Pink has grown up with undertones of gray for a rich look or saturated to a hot pink intensity. Pink always will have a feminine quality and portray your softer side, so care must be taken when using it in rooms for mixed company so that a feminine/masculine balance is achieved.

Purple — Often associated with royalty. Every stage play that needs to portray a king and queen uses deep purple and gold, so if purple is overused in a home it is easy for it to feel "stagey." Use it sparingly to add a rich and dramatic touch to a room.

Black — Not just to designate the "bad guy" in a movie. Black is a fabulous accent in any room and has moved from accent pieces to upholstered pieces and even wall color. When using large amounts of black there is a fine line between rich and luxurious and depressing — be sure to stay away from depressing. Black always will be considered a classic, in both contemporary and traditional looks.

White — Another classic. White feels clean, sleek, and sophisticated and like black can be used in both contemporary and traditional looks. When you are using large amounts of white, it is important to use several different tones and textures to avoid a "boring" look.

Appendix 23: Formal Business Plan Outline

Although a formal business plan is not an absolute necessity in the business of redesign and real estate home staging, understanding the process is not a bad idea. There may come a time that you need to get a loan or decide to go into business with a partner. This appendix will help you create the needed paperwork for these occasions.

Rather than a completed business plan, this appendix will guide you through the different stages of a business plan using questions and sample text. In the end, you will be able to write a business plan that meets all your needs.

Do not feel that you must start at the beginning of the plan. If you have all the information you need to start on the marketing plan or you feel more comfortable starting with a personal finance statement, start there. The only suggestion is to do the executive summary last. Since it is a summary of the plan, you really cannot write this until the entire plan is complete.

Remember, the value of a business plan is not the plan itself. The value comes from the process of the research you performed and the analyses you conducted. By going through this process, you will know more about your business and what you can do to avoid costly errors in the future.

Front Cover

The front cover should contain a title with the name of your company and the words "Business Plan."

Mary Larsen Designs Business Plan

Beneath the title you need to include your business name, your name, other owners' names, your address, your phone number, your fax number, and your e-mail address.

Mary Larsen Designs
Mary Larsen, Owner
3340 Langston Circle
Apex, NC 27539
919-773-1445
mary@marylarsendesigns.com

Executive Summary

An executive summary is a short one- to two-page synopsis of the entire plan. It is easier to write this section last so that you know exactly what is in the rest of the report.

Think of the executive summary the way you would think of a résumé. A résumé lists all your accomplishments and your skills to show potential employers what you have to offer. The executive summary will explain to potential lenders or partners what your company is doing, has done, and has the potential to do. This is your way of getting the best of the best across to readers so that they decide to read on.

Some questions you will want to answer in the executive summary include:

- What is redesign, redecorating, and real estate home staging?

- Who are your customers?

- Who are you, and why do you think you will make a good redesigner?

- What do you think the future holds for your business and your industry?

Additionally, you will want to be explicit in identifying your reason for creating the business plan. For instance, if you are taking the plan to a financial institution in hopes of a loan, the summary should state the amount needed, what the money will be used for, and how the money will help your business. If you wrote it to attract a partner, you will want the executive summary to explain the strengths of the company, why a partner would benefit from the arrangement, and what the expectations of a partnership would be.

General Overview of Your Company

This section will describe your company. You will need to explain what redesign, redecorating, and real estate staging is and exactly what you will do. This section has many subheadings, including:

1. Legal Formation of Your Company

2. Company Mission Statement

3. Business Approach

4. Industry at a Glance

5. Your Company's Strengths

6. Goals

1. Legal Formation of Your Company

How is your company organized? The answer can be one of the following:

- Sole Proprietor

- Partnership

- Corporation

- Limited Liability Corporation

Be sure to explain why you chose this form of organization for your company.

After several years as a sole proprietor, Mary Larsen Designs decided to go with an S corporation because of tax benefits. The primary benefit of an S corporation is that it covers liability and allows the shareholders to receive profits free of taxation at the corporate level. The profits will be taxed only at the individual level.

(See the subheading The Legal End of Business in Chapter 4)

2. Company Mission Statement: A mission statement explains what principles will guide you in your business dealings. Mission statements are best kept to approximately 30 words.

Mary Larsen Designs will work with busy, overworked homeowners who want their home to be a reflection of their successful career. We will do what it takes to fully develop our business and deliver quality professional design services to our clients. The design services delivered are, without exception, our best effort. We adhere to the highest standards of honesty and integrity. Striving for excellence and continuous improvement is part of our business culture and mission.

3. Business Approach

This section helps you explain your approach to your work.

For redesigners, your business approach could be "to make a client's home beautiful and peaceful with little stress."

4. The Industry at a Glance

Those lending you money or considering a partnership will want to understand the industry. This section allows you to tell them about the growth, future changes, and your ability to capitalize on these changes.

5. Your Company's Strengths

No one wants to loan money to a company that will not succeed. A list and explanation of the strengths of your company will help you show potential lenders or partners what your company can do.

When writing this section, be sure to answer the following questions:

- What will make your redesign business successful?

- Considering your competition, what strengths make you stand out?

- What do you bring to the table personally? Do you have a particular skill set or experience that will make this business succeed?

(Chapter 1 will help you answer these questions.)

6. Goals: In this section, you are going to describe your goals and how you will know if you are achieving them.

(See A Simplified Business Plan and SMART Goals in Chapter 3)

Goal: Have a loyal customer base.

Objective: Have five active clients per month.

Products and Services

In this section, you will explain what you will be offering in terms of products and/or services. For example:

Personal shopping: I will shop for my clients after a redesign to purchase items that would make their room look even better.

Patio or porch redesign: I will expand my services out of doors during the spring and summer months.

Holiday and party decorating: I will use my skills to decorate homes for major holidays.

Move-in services: I will help new homeowners decorate after they move into a new home by being there as the movers arrive and putting everything in its place before the client arrives.

Custom window treatments: I will offer window treatments as a way to enhance the value of my client's home. I will work with retail curtains in a way that turns something inexpensive into something that has a more custom look.

Full-service interior design: I will help my clients determine what new furnishings, paint, flooring, and floor plan changes they need and subcontract these services.

Color consultations: I will use my expertise to provide a color consultation so my clients may purchase new furnishing or add color in the form of paint, flooring, or accessories.

Home transitions: I will help clients as they transition from a large house to a small house or a small house to a large house. I also will help elderly clients transition to a retirement community or an assisted living center.

Organizing services: I will help clients clean, declutter, and organize their possessions.

Painting: I will paint clients' walls and ceilings to provide a fresh, new look.

Faux finishing/furniture refinishing: I will use professional techniques to refinish my client's furniture.

Virtual redesign: I will offer computer redesign services, including color selection, custom window treatment ideas, and virtual furniture arrangements.

Interiorscaping: I will help my clients determine their natural plant needs and install these indoor gardens.

You also will want to explain what gives you an advantage over other companies.

ABC Redesign is the only company in the area to focus on children's rooms.

Or

ABC Redesign is the only local business that has shopping as part of the services offered.

Finally, you will want to explain your pricing structure.

(See Chapter 2 for information on services and pricing.)

Marketing Plan

Marketing is imperative to a successful business. Your redesign skills may be second to none, but if no one knows about your company, your company is going to fail. In order to have a good marketing plan, you have to do your research to figure out how to attract your perfect client.

You can gather customer data by using industry literature, such as trade journals, as well as more general information, such as Census material and demographics. An important piece of research is research you gathered on your own. This kind of data is collected through surveys or interviews to find out what your client wants.

The marketing plan has seven subsections. They include:

- Financial Research
- Product/Service Research
- Customer Base Research
- Competition Research
- Niche Research
- Strategy Plan
- Sales Forecast

1. Financial Research

This section deals with the financial facts concerning the redesign, redecorating, and real estate redesign business. In order to determine if your company can succeed in the marketplace, you have to understand the marketplace. This subsection should answer such questions as:

What is the population in the area you will be serving?

ABC Redesign in Sanford, NC, serves an area with a population of 30,000.

How many people in the market area have need of your service?
This can be determined by the number of homes for sale, as well as finding out industry statistics for the percentage of people that use redecorating services.

Is it possible for your business to grow in this market? You can demonstrate this by showing the growth of the area or the current growth of the market or both.

What "barriers to entry" would keep you from entering the marketplace?

Some typical barriers for redesign may be:

- **Marketing costs** — This can be overcome through the use of inexpensive means of advertising, such as free demonstrations, business cards, newsletters, and article writing.

- **Customer acceptance and brand recognition** — Word of mouth, as well as HGTV shows, is helping get the idea of redesign and home staging across to the general public. Writing articles explaining this process while using the Mary Larsen name and logo will help ensure that my company and redesign are synonymous.

- **Training and skills** — Mary Larsen trained at the Virginia Polytechnic Institute and State University, earning a bachelor's degree in clothing and textiles. She worked as an assistant designer for Christian Dior wedding gowns, as well as many years as a Fortune 500 Service Manager. She currently teaches both decorating and business courses and is a featured expert in several books and magazines, as well as a featured designer on *Extreme Makeover: Home Edition*.

You also will explain how changes in the economic environment could affect your business.

For instance, higher mortgage rates and a real estate slowdown can cause a decrease in home staging. However, other services, such as redesign, go up when real estate sales go down. (You would need to show a statistic.)

2. Product/Service Research

In this section, your research concerns what your potential customers will see in your product/service and what benefits they will derive from using your products/services.

For example, in room redesign, the features are:

- Working with a designer, using their skills and talents
- Working with items you have purchased already

Its benefits include:

- You will not need to buy anything new, so the investment is low.
- You get to use the things you already love.
- You get instant gratification in having your room decorated in a day.
- The desire to have your home look "finished" is achieved in one day.

Also list what after-sale services will you give.

(See the subsection Who You Are and What You Do in Chapter 2)

3. Customer Base Research

Demographics include who your customers are, where your customers live, and what they are like. In the redesign/home staging business, it is quite likely that you have more than one customer group.

For instance, you may target redesign to new homeowners and staging to home sellers. Since 80 percent of all moves are within a ten-mile radius, the hope is to have a client who uses both your staging and your redesign services.

For each group, you need to create a demographic profile. Depending on your "perfect" client, the demographics will change. This profile can consist of:

- Age

- Sex

- Location

- Income

- Marital status

- Home ownership

- Etc.

As a redesigner or home stager, you will want to determine the following:

- Are you targeting stay-at-home moms (ages 20 to 40) or

business professionals (ages 35 to 55)?

- Will you market toward women or men? The typical answer is women unless you are targeting couples.

- How far are you willing to travel? This will limit the location of your potential clients.

- How much income do your clients need? You will not sell your redesign services to someone who struggles to meet day-to-day obligations.

4. Competition Research

This subsection helps you identify other companies that compete with you and how they do so. For instance, pure redesigners will compete with you only for those wanting no extra services. They will not be competing with you if you choose to have custom window treatments or shopping as an add-on service.

You also will want to list indirect competitors or those companies whose businesses have services that overlap yours. For instance, are there real estate agents in your area who offer in-house home staging? Are there full-service interior designers who offer redesign?

Finally, you will want to compare your services with those of your competition.

If you lived in Raleigh, NC, you would look under the interior design category of the Yellow Pages. Some of the listings you would see are:

Alice Interiors LLC — Direct competition that does not offer home staging

Allen's Wallpapers — No competition but a source for redesign materials

Angela's Interiors Ltd. — Direct competition in all categories

Architect Designing — Direct competitor in the area of full-service interior design only

Furniture Warehouse — No competition but a source for redesign materials

Homes to Sell Designs — Direct competitor in the area of home staging

Smith Realty — Indirect competition in the area of home staging

5. Niche Research

It is not possible to market to everyone; nor would you want to. Some clients are simply not good for your business. Therefore, after looking at all the different client possibilities, write a short, one-paragraph definition of your niche market.

I will be working with busy, overextended homeowners who do not have much time. Typically the two adults in the home both work. They want their home to reflect the success they have in their career, but they do not have the time to make that happen on their own.

6. Strategic Plan

This plan will show how you will market to your targeted niche.

First, you will need to know how you plan to promote your redesign/home staging service to your niche.

What sort of advertising will you do? How often? Why?

- Print

- Online

- TV

- Radio

What low-cost paid advertising will you use?

- Web site

- Business cards

What no-cost promotions will you use to get the word out?

- Testimonials

- Word of mouth

- Referral programs

- E-mail signatures

- Presentations

- Networking meetings

- Vendor's show

- Silent auctions

- Volunteering

- Writing articles

- Newsletter

- News release

- Radio and TV appearances

What type of graphics will you need for your strategic plan?

- Business cards

- Postcards

- Stationery

- Flyers

- Sign in the yard

Explain your system for keeping up with your clients.

(See the subheading Happy Clients Grow Your Business in Chapter 5, as well as Chapter 9.)

What is the cost associated with your promotional strategy? How much money will you need when the company starts, and how much for ongoing promotional costs?

How will you set your prices? Are your prices competitive? Are your customers likely to shop by price or quality?

(See the subheading You Are Worth It in Chapter 2.)

Explain why your redesign, redecorating, and real estate staging works well from home and does not need a storefront.

A redesign, redecorating, and real estate staging business is perfectly suited for a home office. This business does not require a storefront since the decorator gives consultations in a client's home and does all the hands-on work there as well. Those jobs done off-site, such as choosing color palettes or creating custom window treatments, do not need a storefront.

(See the subheading Home Sweet Office in Chapter 4.)

List the details of receiving a phone call through the consultation process.

(See Chapter 7.)

7. Sales Forecast

A sales forecast is all about the numbers. It is a month-to-month projection of your expenses versus your income. When you make this projection, it should be based on:

- Your historical sales
- Your marketing strategies
- Your market research
- Industry data

Operational Plan

This section gets down to the nuts and bolts of the daily operation of your company. It includes everything from personnel to policy and legalities to light fixtures.

In the operational plan, you will want to describe the legal aspects of your business. This includes licensing, permits, regulations, zoning, insurance, trademarks, and more.

(See the subheading The Legal End of Business in Chapter 4.)

You also will need to describe the personnel involved in your business. Most redesign/home staging companies have the potential for the following:

- Designer — skilled employee

- Administrative assistant — skilled employee

- Laborer to move furniture — unskilled employee

Also include information concerning the use of contract workers, such as contractors, painters, or landscapers.

Inventory is another part of your operational plan. You will need to list the types of inventory you will have on hand and how much you will have invested in the inventory at any given time.

As a redesigner, your inventory might include:

- Accessories

- Furniture

- Fabric

- Paint

- Holiday accessories

Do you have any suppliers? For example, do you distribute for a line of furniture or area rugs? If so, you need to identify this company by name and address. You also will want to list:

- Inventory

- Credit policies

- Responsible nature of the company

Tradle Imports
1234 ABC St.
Raleigh, NC 12345
123-456-7890

Tradle Imports supplies upholstered furniture, including sofas, love seats, and armchairs, as well as wooden end and coffee tables. All furnishings are paid in full before delivery. Tradle Imports delivers to My Designs free of charge or to a client's home for a fee of $75. Tradle Imports has been in operation in Raleigh for 25 years and has an excellent BBB rating.

Another factor to consider is your credit policy. Selling on credit is not the typical industry standard for the redesign/home staging business. Therefore, be sure to mention if you will not be extending credit.

Management and Organization

When a bank lends you money, it wants to know who actually will run the business because this can make a difference in its success or failure. This section explains who runs/manages the business day-to-day and what experience this person has doing so. You also can list any core competencies or skills this person has that are specific to the job at hand.

Finally, you will want to list any members of your support team.

Sean Larsen, Accountant
456 DEF St.
Raleigh, NC
919-555-1234

John Stone, Attorney
789 GHI St.
Raleigh, NC
919-555-5678

Bill Heasley, Insurance Agent
987 JKL St.
Raleigh, NC
919-555-9012

Beth Whitecar
Wachovia
654 MNO St.
Raleigh, NC
919-555-3456

Mary Larsen, Mentor
3340 Langston Cir.
Apex, NC 27539
919-773-1445

Teri B. Clark, Mentor
233 Chris Cole Rd.
Sanford, NC 27332
919-776-9311

Personal Financial Statement

Bankers will need to know what you have personally since you will be using your assets as collateral on your loan. You will need to know your net worth even if you are not getting a loan since you will be using your assets to keep the company afloat in the beginning stages of startup.

Startup Expenses

No matter what business you start, you will incur expenses before you ever open your doors. One of the great things about the redesign/home staging business is that the startup cost is so low. The following are typical items you need to start a redesign/ home staging business:

Pens and pencils — $0 to start (have on hand)

Notepads — $5

File folders — $5

Stapler and staples — $0 to start (have on hand)

Paperclips — $1

Calculator — $0 to start (have on hand)

White out — $1

Printer paper — $10

Business envelopes — $2

Stamps — 41 cents each

Tape — $0 to start (have on hand)

Ruler — $0 to start (have on hand)

Scissors — $0 to start (have on hand)

Self-drilling anchors — $5

Rechargeable cordless drill and batteries — $50

Screwdriver — $0 to start (have on hand)

Wire cutter and various gauges of wire — $15

Stud finder — $10

Sharpie marker — $0 to start (have on hand)

Straight and safety pins — $0 to start (have on hand)

Rubber bands — $0 to start (have on hand)

Museum or poster putty — $5

Furniture touch-up sticks or pens — $5

Floral sheers and tape — $5

Painter's tape — $5

Glue gun and sticks — $0 to start (have on hand)

Lint brush and wrinkle-release spray — $10

Flashlight — $0 to start (have on hand)

Spackling putty — $5

Masking tape and Scotch tape — $0 to start (have on hand)

Furniture sliders — $25

Mark-it level — $25

Be sure to explain how you came up with the item list and expenses associated with these items.

(See Chapter 4, Setting Up Shop.)

Financial Plan

Just as you had to have a marketing plan, you will need to have a financial plan. The plan will show your expected profits and losses for the first year and over four years, a projection of cash flow, a projected balance sheet, and, finally, what it will take to break even.

These projections will help you predict your company's future.

12-Month Profit and Loss Projection

A 12-month profit and loss projection puts all the numbers together to give you an idea of what it will take to make a profit. This is done on a month-by-month basis as you forecast the following:

- Sales

- Cost of products sold

- Expenses

- Profits

In addition to a spreadsheet with these items, it is a good idea to use a narrative to explain how you came to these particular estimations.

For example, if you predict that you will make $2,000 a month for the first 12 months of the year, you have to explain how you came up with that number. In this case, it could be that you have been able to redesign two to three rooms per month at a profit of $500 a room prior to promoting your business. You believe that your marketing will help you gain one to two clients per month.

Projected Cash Flow

A business is unsuccessful when it runs out of money. A projected cash flow can help you foresee such an event.

Your projected cash flow will include:

- Startup money
- Operating expenses
- Reserves

Opening-Day Balance Sheet

This is just a spreadsheet that shows your company's assets versus its debts. When you subtract your debts from your assets, you get your equity. For most redesign/home staging businesses, little debt is incurred, so your assets and your equity will be nearly the same.

Break-Even Analysis

This is a prediction of what you will have to do in sales to cover your costs. It gives numbers to what it will take to operate at a profit.

Appendices

You can complete your business plan by using appendices. These can include such things as:

- Your promotional materials
- Industry studies

Report Date
Spring 2007

Nearest Metro Area
Raleigh/Durham/Chapel Hill

Buyers' or Sellers' Market?
Equal buyers and sellers

Average Time on Market
60 to 90 days

Market Trend
Increasing

Housing Inventory
Good supply — all prices

Average Home Prices
$275,000

Compared to last year
Up 0 to 5 percent

Prices as Percent of Asking Price
95 to 100 percent

Multiple Offers?
Yes

Greatest Activity
Single-family homes

Housing Hot Spots
North Raleigh/Cary

Reason to Buy/Sell
Good economic news

Author Biography

*M*ary Larsen is an established, nationally recognized interior decorating professional committed to developing design professionals through **www.GrowYourDesignBiz.com** — Designing Your Success™. She has taught decorating and business courses to women's groups and "trade only" conferences throughout the nation. Mary has been featured in industry trade publications as an industry expert and is a contributing writer for the Raleigh *News & Observer* and the *Cary News*. Her decorating business focuses on window treatments and room redesign.

Mary has had the distinct pleasure of working on the Raleigh 2007 home on ABC's *Extreme Makeover: Home Edition*. Her work was featured on the show, as well as on the ABC *Extreme Makeover: Home Edition* Web site. She is also a featured designer in Teri B. Clark's real estate staging book *301 Simple Things*. This is Mary's first book.

Mary is a popular speaker with an enthusiastic, contagious spirit, and she easily shows others the possibilities for their own businesses. If you are looking for training classes or more personal consulting for your new redesign or home staging business, you can find it at **www.GrowYourDesignBiz.com**. Mary can be reached by visiting **www.MaryLarsenDesigns. com** or **www.GrowYourDesignBiz.com**.

If you have enjoyed this book, please visit **www. GrowYourDesignBiz.com/gift** for a thank you gift from Mary.

Index